The Way to True
WORSHIP

A Popular Story of Hinduism

Anoop Chandola

UNIVERSITY
PRESS OF
AMERICA

Lanham • New York • London

Copyright © 1991 by
University Press of America®, Inc.
4720 Boston Way
Lanham, Maryland 20706

3 Henrietta Street
London WC2E 8LU England

Library of Congress Cataloging-in-Publication Data

Chandola, Anoop.
The way to true worship : a popular story of Hinduism
/ by Anoop Chandola.
p.   cm.
Includes translation of: Satyanarayanavratakatha.
Includes bibliographical references and index.
1. Puranas.   Skandapurana.   Revakhanda.
Satyanarayanavratakatha—Criticisim, interpretation, etc.
I. Puranas.   Skandapurana.   Revakhanda.
Satyanarayanavratakatha. English. 1991.
II. Title.
BL1140.4.S5342R4833   1991
294.5'925—dc20   90–49366 CIP

ISBN 0–8191–8047–5 (cloth : alk. paper)
ISBN 0–8191–8048–3 (pbk.: alk. paper)

To my mother, KISHORI DEVI, and my father, SATYA PRASAD—my first teachers of the priestly profession

Contents

Preface

In Madison, during the summer of 1973 when my wife and I were teaching at the University of Wisconsin, a north Indian friend invited us to a Hindu worship in his home, with his family and friends. The ceremony performed was to be the Satya Narayana Vrata Katha, which is Sanskrit for *The True God Worship Story*.

With an "insider's" knowledge of practical Hinduism, I was aware that this worship is very popular among Hindus. But I was initially incredulous to learn that it was widely practiced in the United States by Hindus with American college degrees.

A priest, who was going to perform the ceremony, was indeed a graduate from a university here. His style of worship was slightly different from mine because he came from the south of India and I from the extreme north, the central Himalayas (between Badrinath and Rishikesh). He performed the rites in Sanskrit most authentically. Children were given explanations in English as were many adult Hindus who did not know Sanskrit. After the worship, our host and hostess had a fine party for us, and we all happily spent more than four hours in their home.

The following week I met my host friend and thanked him for inviting me, with my wife and son, to the worship. Moreover I wished him success in the fulfillment of whatever wish he had in mind on that occasion. I told him that indeed my own wish had been fulfilled—that two days earlier I had received an unexpected phone call from the Anthropology Program of the National Science Foundation. The news was that I had been awarded a big grant that I had applied for a second time.

Following this experience, I was to become acquainted with more and more Hindu families living in the United States and performing this worship. I asked myself this question: Why do Hindus like this particular worship so much?

One answer is that they believe in the efficacy of the worship—in its miraculous powers to bring about fulfillment of their wishes sooner than expected. But this obvious conclusion did not satisfy my need for understanding.

vii

The Satya Narayana Vrata Katha is, I realized, not a worship only, but a family and community activity. It is not a part of any regular cycle of ceremonies or of the organized religion. It can be performed by anyone, at any time, and in any place–in versions short or long, in Sanskrit or any other language. Viewed in this regard, the worship is adaptable, flexible, portable, and in all such ways suited to the fast-paced, highly mobile life of modern people.

Hindus have especially high regard for its educational aspects: it teaches them how to view God, how to worship and how to find mythological support for their worship–several valuable elements of continuity for a religion exposed to a changing world.

It seemed more than ever paradoxical, then, that a worship so popular has had no English translation until this volume. The end result of my pondering was the writing of this book, which provides not only simple translation of the original text but also complete description of the worship itself. Here and there, I have added social, behavioral, symbolic, philosophical, and literary explanations to help the reader understand why the worship and its stories are even more popular among Hindus than the *Bhagavad Gita*.

I have tried to avoid scholarly jargon for two reasons: first, because this book is addressed to a wide audience; and second (as mentioned earlier) I have written this book, not just as a scholar, but from an insider's perspective. Above all, I have tried to present a new and simple way for the reader to understand how religious activities can make sense to their performers and believers.

I am grateful more than I can say, to individuals and institutions for their help with this book. I want to thank the University of Arizona for granting sabbatical leave in the Fall of 1987 for analysis of my fieldwork in India.

While in the field, I worked with several priests (Brahmins), some of them relatives. Among these my special thanks go to Janardan Prasad Silmana, Krishna Prasad Gautam (of Nepal), Ramakrishna Bahuguna, Chandra Mani Juyal, and Mohan Kothyal. I am grateful also to Edgar Polome, Paul Turner, and Joseph Elder for several kinds of help in the past.

I would also like to thank several other friends for their free services, especially the following. Shakuntala Deshwar drew the mandala and K.H. Dehwar provided additional material on the *Skanda Purana*. The photographs from the puja performed at the Tucson home of Neena and

Mradul Mehrotra were taken by Kewal Parnami and Sudesh Chawla. The Ganesha photograph was provided by Swaran Singh Chima from New Delhi.

Thanks also to Elizabeth Shaw for editing, Hanni Forester for the miniature painting, Janis Prochaska for calligraphy and artwork on the mandala, and Barbara Cook for preparing the final press copy.

Finally I thank Sudha, my wife, and Varn, my son, for their cooperation and encouragement throughout the preparation of the book.

Anoop Chandola

श्रीसत्यनारायणव्रतकथा

ॐ लक्ष्मीनारायणाभ्यां नमः

Vishnu Anantashayin
(Miniature painting, late 19th century, Kashmir, India)
ASIAN ART MUSEUM OF SAN FRANCISCO, The Avery Brundage Collection (86 D15)

Introduction

Today more than a half-billion Hindus, in India and around the globe, share a common core of worship that employs the Vedic mantras from the second millennium B.C. to the Puranic tradition of medieval times. Since the 1960s, there has been a growing interest in practical Hinduism, indicated by popular movements, college courses, and attention to the subject in nonscholarly periodicals and other media of the Western world. Yet from the practitioner's point of view, the worship itself, which is the modus operandi of Hinduism, has been left largely undocumented, untranslated, and unexplained.

This volume contains the first English translation of the *Satya Narayana Vrata Katha* or "The True God Worship Story." It includes authentic description and explanation of the procedures, techniques, materials, mantras, prayers, myths, concepts, and symbols associated with that worship.

It is understood in traditional societies that people engage in worship mainly because they wish to have their needs and desires met, not only surely but rapidly. Hindu worshippers are no exception. This is evidenced by contemporary use of the ancient Vedic mantras recorded in Sanskrit in the *Satya Narayana Vrata Katha*.

Satya, the first term in the Sanskrit title, derives from *sat*, which is among the most frequently used words in Indian religious literature. The first recorded book of the Hindus is the *Rig Veda*. In it, "being" or *sat* is said to have its beginning in non-being or *asat*. More than a thousand years later, the *Bhagavad Gita* challenged this view, holding that there is no "non-being" state of being. In the evolution of the term and the concept by medieval times, the worship of Satya Narayana had become identified with the ancient Vishnu, to emerge as a means by which the "common" people could bring things into being from a state of non-being. After another millennium, in the twentieth century, Mahatma Gandhi used *sat* in naming his movement of nonviolence and civil disobedience—*Satyagraha* or "Truth's force." Gandhi believed that God was Truth, or *satya*.

Meaning of the term differs greatly with the diversity of systems and semantics. The *Bhagavad Gita*, for example, advocates "desireless action," whereas the Satya Narayana worship is performed mainly in order to fulfill the worshipper's desire.

Mahatma Gandhi, like the Vedic Aryans, did not believe in worshipping images. The Satya Narayana believer maintains philosophically that any existing form or *sat*, be it word or object, can be a communicative symbol for God, who is also non-form or *asat* and is ultimately beyond either *sat* or *asat*. To the believer, things may make sense only when they can be imaged or materialized or conceptualized. This point will be clarified later in the book.

The other key word in the worship is *Narayana*. In classical Hindu mythology, Brahma, the Creator, was born in a lotus that emerged from the milky cosmic ocean. He became eager to find the source of his origin. He searched in all four directions, and in the attempt he developed four heads as well as four arms, but nowhere did he find his progenitor. He then descended the lotus stalk into the cosmic waters but here also, for thousands of years, he did not find the source of the lotus. Its root was lodged in the navel of Narayana who dwelt in the waters on the body of the "Infinite" Ananta, actually Narayana's "Remainder," or Shesha. How could Brahma react to such a being, whose remainder was infinite?

Brahma came up from the cosmic ocean resolved to practice penance and meditation, which led him to see Narayana within himself. Following this realization, he began his work: creation.

Hence, the Hindu meaning of the word Narayana is the "One whose residence is waters." Waters are the symbol of that from which all life grows; and here we see Hinduism sharing a concept not only with other great religions but with Western scientific thought about the origins of life.

In Hindu worship, water is the first thing to be offered the deity; then seeds, other fluids, leaves, flowers, and fruits, in that order. At the end, after music has been played or sung, the fruits, considered to be God's grace, are distributed among the participants, to be consumed with other sacred food and drink.

Here we see the ritualistic fertilization and fructification of new life–the worshipper's wishes sanctified and also a human fellowship so that the celebration of life can be shared.

Comparing this view of life to that presented in the *Gita* presents a paradox. In the *Gita*, Krishna tells Arjuna that one should take action with no desire for the fruit of this action. In the True God Worship Story, Narayana (Vishnu) tells Narada, a compassionate wanderer and devotee of

Vishnu, how one may worship for the fulfillment of his or her desires. Krishna, in the *Gita*, is an avatar or incarnation of Vishnu. The *Gita* was prepared for an "elitist" audience; beings, for example, such as Arjuna, the princely warrior. The True God Worship Story, by contrast, is meant for "common" people who are said to become active only when there is an incentive. The paradox is that both of these ways of being active are accredited to Vishnu. Semantically there is no difference between them. Vishnu, "all-pervading," means also "one who is active," which is the common meaning of both worships.

If, indeed, the message of the True God Worship Story is that one must take action to achieve gains, then this is clearly a "capitalistic" tale. But for the worshipper, this capitalistic spirit must be balanced by an ethical socialism–or sharing based on what Western capitalistic philosophy would call "enlightened self-interest." In short, this basis for sharing wealth is not a mandated collectivism but is essentially, altruism. Vishnu is interested in everyone's well being. This is the primary concern of Narada as it appears in the beginning of the text.

"Sharing" is the literal meaning of *bhakti*, although "devotion" is the main connotation. The determining concept through the True God Worship is that this worship and all associated activities take place within the concept of *bhakti*.

As learned in this worship, the individual good and the good of society are brought into harmonious balance. When this balance is disturbed, misery is the result. Some characters in the religious tales disturb this balance and get into serious trouble. Eventually their misery is over when they realize the true meaning of worship.

In fact, the translation of the True God Worship Story, although essential, is only one part of this volume. Three other parts or sections support the meaning of the text and how it works in practice. I do not use the word, "support" in a missionary or proselytizing sense but as amplification.

Part I explains the religious literary history that is the background for the worship text. Part II explains how other Hindu philosophical and mythological aspects are related to the worship and the stories. Part III is the translation, which will be simpler to follow after absorbing the first two parts. Part IV explains exactly how the entire performance takes place.

The support system for the translation includes other explanatory devices such as a pronunciation guide to Sanskrit words, a glossary, and a bibliography as a guide to further reading. The volume also contains, besides translation of the central text for the True God Worship Story, translation of such associated material as mantras, prayers, hymns, and other religious verses. There are, of course, previous English versions of many of these, but since a word or sentence can often be translated in more than one way, I have provided my own versions for the sake of contextuality.

PART I

THE LITERARY BACKGROUND

Ganesha

THE ANCIENT HINDU LITERATURE

The roots of Hinduism are so old and so diverse that any attempt to date them historically would be wishful at best. Experts know that the enormous body of Hindu literature is the largest in the world. To be able to classify its parts and translate them into English or any other major modern language is an achievement often dreamed and never realized.

The following references and statements are intended to form a small and yet representative image of Hindu literature. Starting with the earliest-known prayers may serve this purpose. The Indo-European people who began to enter the Indian subcontinent from Iran and Afghanistan before 1500 B.C. called themselves Aryans, not Hindus. Their Indo-European language, rich in oral literature, was called Sanskrit. Their religion was polytheistic, with both gods and goddesses.

After they were well settled in the northwestern region, the Aryan priests collected the oral verse in a book known as the *Rig Veda*. Each of the ten volumes, probably completed over several hundred years, was called a *mandala*, meaning "circle," or "round," or "collection." The word *rig* is a phonetic variation of *richa* or *rich*, which means "verse" or *mantra*. *Veda* means "knowledge." *Rig Veda*, therefore, is the first book of Aryan knowledge in the Vedic dialect of Sanskrit, an archaic form differing from standard Sanskrit.

The *Rig Veda* provides information on the early religious and secular life of the Aryans. Their religious rituals and ceremonies were referred to by the term *yajna*. In a *yajna*, mantras were recited with rituals to please the gods and goddesses. The hymns of the *Rig Veda*, thus, are the first known prayers of the Aryan people. Three more Vedas were added: *Yajur Veda*, *Sama Veda*, and *Atharva Veda*. The Vedas are called *shrutis*; that is, they were heard as heard by others through oral transmission. To the four Vedas were attached later some secondary books called *Brahmanas, Aranyakas*, and *Upanishads*.

The religious tenets and practices of the early Aryans begin with the *Rig Veda* and end around 1,000 B.C. with the *Upanishads*, which are not only the last parts of the Vedic literature but deal also with the knowledge of Self, especially the realization of the individual *atman* or "self" as a single Universal Self or *Brahman*. The early Aryans considered self-realization the ultimate goal or "end" of human life. The *Upanishads* are called the books of *Vedanta* (from *veda* "knowledge," and *anta* "end.")

On the Indian subcontinent, the Aryans found three non-Aryan peoples already resident: the Austrics (or Austro-Asiactics), the Dravidians, and the Tibeto-Burmans. Through contact, the Aryans and non-Aryans began to modify and integrate each other's pathways. In the context of religion, for example, the Austro-Asiatics may have contributed the belief in each life passing to another life. This belief later, in the form of reincarnation, became a major element in the *Upanishads*. The Dravidians are conjectured to have added such aspects as yoga, *puja* ("honor" or "worship," especially image worship), vegetarianism, and several deities including Shiva and Mother Goddess Uma. Also there was a pre-Aryan Indus Valley civilization whose religious practices included a godlike figure resembling Shiva.

The diverse and ancient peoples of the region expressed their strong need for a pluralistic view of religion very early in the *Rig Veda*, as indicated by the *mantra*:

> *ekam sad viprā bahudhā vadanti*
> "The wise speak of the one True in many ways."

The word, *sad*, is a phonetic variation of *sat*, meaning "true" or "truth." The search for truth in many different ways became the guideline for the evolution of religion among the multiracial, multisocial people that outsiders called Hindus.

The word "Hindu" was used for the river Sindhu by the old Persian speakers of Iran. The Greeks received the word from the Persians and pronounced it *Indu*, calling the river Indus and the land India. Around this river the Aryans encountered a more advanced people, but the Persians called them all Hindus, whether Aryan or non-Aryan.

The ancient "Indians," although they did not refer to themselves as Hindus or their religion as Hinduism, were aware of their religion's ancient roots and hence called it *sanatana*, meaning "senior," or "everlasting," or "perpetuating."

Gradually they began to experience changes of various sorts. Major change, for example, came in the pronunciation and grammar of the Vedic speech, which was an archaic dialect of Sanskrit. The mode of transmission of Vedic literature was oral-aural. Hindu tradition held that an editor named Vyasa ("arranger," or "editor") organized the Vedic mantras as "seen" by the seers or *Rishis*. Yet, in the historical sense, a priestly class was responsible for the collection of the Vedas as books.

The Vedic society was divided into four *varnas* or classes. In the class called *Brahmana* (Brahmins) were the priests and scholars. The *Kshatriyas* or *Rajanyas* were the rulers, including the military; the business class was called *Vaishya*, and the labor, *Shudra*. The priests, or Brahmins, were the ones concerned about preservation of the ancient religion.

From this concern, another body of literature called *Vedanga* was developed before 500 B.C. There were six categories of this literature that dealt mainly with linguistic and ritual aspects. These included rules of pronunciation, grammar, metrics, etymology, and information about celestial bodies and mathematics. Some of these texts and procedures appear in books generically called *Sutras* ("formulas" or "aphorisms"). The *Grihya Sutras* include sacraments used within the structure of family or home. The nondomestic sutras are known as *Shrauta* and *Dharma Sutras*, and they deal respectively with Vedic rituals and public conduct. The most important Sanskrit grammar, the *Ashtadhyayi*, authored by Panini soon after 500 B.C., is also in the sutras. With this grammar, the Sanskrit language became standardized.

Sutra literature may have begun before 600 B.C. By this time the Aryan religion, with its *yajnas* and the Dravidian religion with its *puja* were practiced in tandem at home and in public under the guidance of priests. The so-called Sanatana Dharma now had its traditions from two major sources of ancient times: the Aryan and the Dravidian. This process of including more and more traditions was to continue throughout the history of Hinduism.

THE GREAT EPICS

The Vedas included several major gods and goddesses some of whom must have been culture heroes. Among the most popular deities were Agni, Indra, Varuna, Vishnu, Prajapati, Rudra, Surya, Yama, etc. As the tradition of honoring culture heroes continued, in due course new heroes were added, two of them most important: Rama and Krishna.

The first Sanskrit epics are two ancient and great works: the *Ramayana* and the *Mahabharata*. Rama is the hero in the *Ramayana*, authored by Valmiki. Krishna is celebrated in the *Mahabharata*, believed to have been the work of Vyasa. Considering their formidable size, it is clear that these epics each evolved over several hundred years. The characters in the

Ramayana, Prince Rama and his wife Princess Sita, already might have been popular earlier than Buddha, a culture hero whose time is historically verifiable (*ca.* 563-483 B.C.). The other great hero in that era was Mahavira, probably a contemporary of Buddha and one of the founders of Jainism. In the Hindu tradition Valmiki is considered to be a contemporary of Rama. But the actual, available form of the *Ramayana* seems to have been completed long after the death of both Buddha and Mahavira.

Many modern scholars believe that the *Mahabharata* must have existed before the *Ramayana*. Certainly its more than one hundred thousand verses (mainly couplets) were completed long after Buddha's time, and it is indeed the longest epic in the world.

In the Hindu view, Rama is an avatar or avatara "descent" or "incarnation" of Vishnu who preceded Krishna, another avatar. The concept of avatar appears clearly for the first time in the *Mahabharata*. The story basically is a fight between cousins named Kauravas and Pandavas, in which Krishna helps Pandavas. The eighteen chapters of the *Mahabharata* called the *Gita* ("song") form a famous philosophical discourse that occurs just as the two armies are ready to fight, between Krishna and Arjuna who is one of the five Pandava brothers. Krishna tells Arjuna to perform action without desire for its reward. He further states that he assumes form to protect *dharma* and the innocent. The various context meanings of *dharma* include among others: way, moral code, ethical conduct, righteousness, norm, fairness, law, order, and behavior.

Desireless action (*nishkama karma*) and the abstract Supreme Divine's concrete manifestation as avatar are the two notable contributions of the *Gita*. The notion of avatar is considered significant in *bhakti* or the philosophy of devotion; but socially, it is a device to integrate diverse communities or groups by recognizing their culture heroes and their contributions. Acceptance of an avatar means social willingness to accept new pathways found under the leadership of a charismatic person. In this manner an outdated *dharma* or way could be abandoned or changed. As is said elsewhere in the *Mahabharata:*

"Path is that which the great person went by."

These "great persons" were not seen as in conflict with one another, even though their paths might conflict. People were taught to believe that these persons were diverse expressions of one and the same Supreme Being or the One Truth.

The great epics demonstrated belief not in drastic but gradual changes within a well-defined social and individual life. This is evidenced by the epics' general support for the *varnashrama* dharma inherited from the ancestral religion. The four *varnas,* once again, are Brahmana, Kshatriya, Vaishya, and Shudra. The four *ashramas* are four stages of individual life: *brahmacharya, grihastha, vanaprastha,* and *samnyasa.* These refer to the lives of student, householder, retiree, and renunciate respectively as an individual life passes from childhood to old age.

Besides these social and individual divisions of life, four goals of life are supported by the great epics. These are: *dharma, artha, kama,* and *moksha.* The term covering the four is *purushartha,* meaning "man's meanings" or "human goals." *Dharma* is ethical conduct including private and public norms applied with a sense of fairness to all. *Artha* refers to earthly or worldly "earning" for livelihood; *kama* refers to material pleasures or desires. The last goal, *moksha,* or "release" is most important as it intends to give freedom from rebirth.

THE DARSHANAS, SMRITIS, AND TANTRAS

After Buddha and before the first century A.D., we find the religious and philosophical systems known by the term, *Darshana* or "view." In fact, the roots are much older than this. For example the yoga described in Patanjali's *Yoga Darshana* is anticipated by the *Upanishads.* But when the followers of Buddha and Mahavira began to develop the nontheistic or atheistic Buddhist and Jaina Darshanas, the Brahmins came up with six major Darshanas, some theistic and some nontheistic. For example, the *Nyaya* is a theistic school, but *Sankhya* is nontheistic. Thus it is clear from the Darshanas that the so-called Hinduism includes theistic as well as nontheistic schools. The best-known materialist nontheistic school is the *Charvaka Darshana.*

Between the first and fourth centuries A.D., another class of literature gained significance in the form of code or law books, referred to as *Smritis* ("that which is remembered", "tradition"). The *Shrutis* (Vedas) and the *Smritis* are joined in the context of the so-called *Sanatana Dharma.*

From this time on a parallel but "counterstandard" class of religious literature began to gain popularity. Traditionally it was called *agama* and differentiated from the standard *nigama* "Vedic" literature. The term *tantra* is also used for *agama,* although not all *tantras* include tantric or mystical practices. In sectarian terms they are categorized in three ways: Vaishnava, Shaiva, and Shakta. Another classification is *dakshina* "right," and *vama* "left," which correspond to good and bad practices. For example, the Vaishnava tantras known as the *Vaikhanasa* and the *Pancharatra* are considered "good" socially. But the Shaiva and Shakta tantras include both good and bad.

THE OLD MYTHOLOGIES

The Puranic period of Hinduism followed the Smriti. The period is named after the Sanskrit word, *purana,* meaning ancient. The word is Vedic, referring to a body of literature different from the Vedas. The *Atharva Veda* (*ca.* 1000 B.C.) mentions Puranic literature coexisting with the Vedas, but the Sanskrit in which all the Puranas are found is not the archaic variety known as Vedic but follows the grammatical rules of Panini. In the Puranic list of the major avatars there is the Buddha avatar, which tells us that the Puranic literature is definitely post-Buddhistic or post-Paninian. The Puranas, moreover, draw on the great epics and Smritis. Most scholars believe that some Puranic contents may be older, but their clear emergence is observed after the third or fourth century A.D. After this, we see a continuous tradition of this genre, extending to the sixteenth or seventeenth century A.D.

Puranas are ranked as *mahapurana* (major) or *upapurana* (minor). The total is thirty-six or more, depending upon how a post-Vedic mythological work is interpreted. In the tradition of the Sanskrit lexicographer, Amara Simha, the Puranas contain five features: creation, recreation, genealogical description of the deities, cosmic time periods or intervals of the Manus, and genealogical description of the kings. The *Bhagavata Purana* lists five more: activities, protection, salvation, being, and Supreme Being.

In reality, the material in the Puranas defies classification on this basis. The Puranic literature is in fact an encyclopedia of Hindu culture as practiced from the fourth century A.D. It contains information on the various major male and female deities and their holy places; the stories of their importance; the rituals to be performed in their honor; and associated religious paraphernalia. The most important deities are Brahma, Vishnu, and Shiva—the Hindu triad representing the cycle of creation, preservation, and dissolution. The Puranas are sometimes divided according to the importance given to one of these three deities in a Purana, but there are Puranas in which the *Devi* or female deity dominates. Another tradition, perhaps the simplest, groups the eighteen major Puranas by their first letters. The list below includes the eighteen Puranas in alphabetical order.

Agni, Bhagavata, Bhavishya, Brahma, Brahmanda, Brahmavaivarta, Garuda, Kurma, Linga, Markandeya, Matsya, Narada, Padma, Skanda, Vamana, Varaha, Vayu, Vishnu.

Some add two more Puranas as major ones, namely the *Devi* and the *Shiva.* Among the eighteen or so minor Puranas the following are noteworthy:

Brihaddharma, Bhargava, Kalika, Kalki, Mahabhagavata, Maheshvara, Narasimha, Parashara, Samba, Sanatkumara, Varuna, Vishnudharma, Vishnudharmottara.

The *Harivamsha* is sometimes included also as a Purana attached to the *Mahabharata.* Our main interest here is in the *Skanda Purana*, the largest of all.

THE SKANDA PURANA

Like other Puranas, this one is largely in the *shloka* meter, a popular and easy style of couplet called also *anushtubh*, which has either four quarters with eight syllables each or two lines with sixteen syllables each. This Purana contains between 80,000 and 100,000 couplets or two lines of verse. This large number results from the variety of associated texts. The enormous size of the *Skanda* is explained also by it having been started probably as early as A.D. 700 and not completed in present from until A.D. 1300.

As indicated earlier, the major Puranas are classified in sectarian terms also; mainly as the Shaiva and Vaishnava sects, with central deities respectively Shiva and Vishnu. Such a classification should not be taken literally because there is a good deal of overlapping in the Puranas. The *Skanda,* for example, is traditionally considered, as the name suggests, to be a Shaiva Purana. One of the sons of Shiva and Parvati is named Skanda. A Vishnu ritual, however, such as the one discussed below, can be found in this Purana of Shiva, which says clearly that Shiva and Vishnu are one and the same. The contents dealing with Shiva do, however, constitute the bulk of this Purana.

The inclination in the Purana to integrate the Shaivite and Vaishnavite differences relates to the concept of *mandala* (or circle or collection, as in the name for the volumes of the *Rig Veda*). The purpose of mandala is to collect and organize a number of entities in one place, assuming that they are in contact with each other by means of their roles or functions. Ritualistically a mandala is a seating arrangement of the various deities. Usually a circle is drawn in which each deity has a particular place. A round metal plate instead of a drawn circle is also used. The main deity is seated in the center with other selected deities placed around it. Those who would worship the nucleus or central deity must first worship the satellites, a procedure very common in Hindu worship.

Underlying this mandalic procedure is the concept that can be called "multimonotheism." In this concept one deity is the central or main deity and the others are supporting deities. The "many" lead the worshipper to the "one"–hence, the multimonotheistic term applies. This is why a *puja* or worship is named after the central deity, even though several others are included. The *puja* performed in this manner is considered to move force to and focus on the central deity, while recognizing the importance of the supporting deities in the movement of such a force.

The reverse of multimonotheism is monomultitheism. The Upanishadic view refers to the monomultitheistic movement by saying that "That One said in the beginning: I (am) one, (let me) be many (*eko'ham bahu syāma*)." The *puja* symbolizes such an expansion or evolution from singular to plural. Before the *puja* begins, the worshipper sips or sprinkles water with the name or mantra of Vishnu–the one main deity. Then several deities come forth for their share of honor before Vishnu is worshipped. The *puja* ends with the farewell of all the deities. The last deity to receive farewell from the worshipper is Vishnu, the Satya Narayana. Thus, in the dynamics of *puja* is clearly observed the divine cycle of "singular to plural" and "plural to singular" symbolized respectively by the dynamic notions of monomultitheism and multimonotheism.

Interestingly enough, these notions suit the politics of the pluralistic or multiethnic Indian society. The relative share of honor or recognition accorded to each deity means that a deity with a minor role in one ritual can have a major role in another.

The contents of the *Skanda Purana* are divided into sections and subsections referred to by the term *khanda* (section or region or part) of which the following are considered authentic.

Section	Sub-section
1. *Maheshvara:*	*Kedara, Kaumarika, Arunachala*
2. *Vishnu:*	*Venkatachala, Purushottamakshetra, Badarikashrama, Karttikamasa, Margashirshamasa, Bhagavata, Vaishakhamasa, Ayodhya*
3. *Brahma:*	*Setu, Dharmaranya, Uttara*
4. *Kashi*	
5. *Avanti:*	*Avantikshetra, Chaturashitilinga, Reva*
6. *Nagara*	
7. *Prabhasa:*	*Prabhasakshetra, Vastrapathakshetra, Arbuda, Dvaraka*

As these divisions suggest, the main theme of the *Skanda* is description of the holy places related to Shiva and Vishnu. No other Sanskrit work is believed to have such detail of the holy places so abundant in India. Each description includes associated stories and rituals to be performed at various times.

THE MOST POPULAR CHAPTERS

In this book we will focus on *Revakhanda,* a subsection of the *Skanda.* The river Narmada in central India is called *Reva* also, and this subsection deals with the importance of the Reva Region or Reva Khanda. Subsumed here is a group of five chapters making up the text of a Vishnu ritual with its associated stories. This text is extracted from the *Skanda,* with the following title: Satya Narayana Vrata Katha, four words that can be translated this way: *Satya* "truth" or "true"; *Narayana* "Vishnu, God"; *Vrata* "vow or worship"; and *Katha* "story."

From a performance point of view, the title suggests two parts: Vrata "worship" and Katha "story." The worship part is described briefly in the first chapter, followed by other chapters that contain stories or episodes showing the significance of the worship. If the performance is to be elegant and elaborate, a priest is needed. The Sanskrit texts with their translations in a modern regional language, prefaced with priestly procedures in Sanskrit, comprise a manual or handbook for the purpose of performing this ritual.

A professional priest does not derive his knowledge from such a handbook; in fact, his procedures go beyond any typical handbook. A body of Sanskrit literature called *Nibandha* was developed just after the Puranas began to dominate Hindu life. The *Nibandha* was followed by the *Paddhati*. A modern Hindu priest bases his knowledge mainly on the Nibandhas and Paddhatis, which combine procedures from the Vedic down to the Puranic style and treat of the various rites, rituals, ceremonies, and sacraments. In the elaborate performance of the Satya Narayana Vrata Katha ritual by a professional priest are touches ranging from the Vedas to the Puranas.

Several concepts and characters that appear in the text and in the procedures need explanation. The two most important concepts are *katha* and *puja,* which this entire work sees as within the concept of *bhakti* or devotion. For convenience, I will use the term "Worship" to refer to the *puja* texts and the term "Story" to refer to the five chapters of the *Skanda* section in the *Reva Khanda*. This usage conforms to the way they are popularly referenced in the context of this ritual.

It should be noted that the Story and Worship concern only one deity; namely, Satya Narayana. As mentioned earlier, in a Hindu *puja,* there are several supporting or satellite deities that must be honored, even though briefly, along with the main or nucleus deity.   Because of its monomultitheistic and multimonotheistic nature, the *puja* becomes highly "enriched." This means also that I will have to include here several more explanations for the various deities as well.

This book shows us a major mythology in action and how it is understood and expressed in the daily lives of the Hindus. Here the term "mythology" may not be quite appropriate. The Hindu tradition considers all Puranic works part of its literature, to be "used" for religious purposes. The users are meant to be "common people." For them, the language must be simple and straightforward, even when expressed in verse. It is because of the simple language of the Puranas that their contents can be part of the chain of activities in the user's mundane life. Literary niceties could have been obstacles when performance was the goal of the contents.

The five chapters translated here illustrate the philosophy of the Puranic literary tradition which presents a twofold requirement, with both elements being essential for effective ritual performance: the context of daily activity and the presence of those who believe—without which no ritual will make sense.

PART II

CONCEPTS AND CHARACTERS

A Satya Narayana puja: The priest on the left directing the husband and wife in their worship.

THE BIG GODS

In the Worship or *puja* are honored the five most important deities, *pancha devas* (*pancha* "five," *deva* "deity"). These are Ganesha, Gauri, Shiva, Surya and Vishnu. The central deity in the present *puja* is Vishnu. In another *puja* some other deity, e.g., Lakshmi, goddess of fortune and wife of Vishnu, may be central, and the *pancha devas* still appear as the supporting deities. A *puja* of Lakshmi is celebrated during the Festival of Lights (*Dipavali*), which falls in the eighth Hindu month (*Karttika* or October-November). A brief mythological description of Ganesha, Gauri, Shiva, and Surya follows:

GANESHA

Of all five deities Ganapati or Ganesha is the most important; a *puja* or project is begun with his name and prayer and is longer than the *pujas* of other supporting deities for he is "lord of the attendants." In this or any *puja*, rapid fulfillment of the worshipper's wish is possible if there are no obstacles. Ganesha is worshipped first because he is the "obstacle remover" (*Vighnahara*), a purpose he is aided in serving by his troops or attendants, the *ganas*.

Ganesha's mother is Parvati and his father Shiva. His older brother is Skanda for whom the *Skanda Purana* is named, hence a Shaiva Purana. Ganesha's images or pictures show him as a human body with an elephant head. Concerning this unique form there are two stories worth noting.

In one, Shiva and Parvati assumed the elephant form for a period during which a son was born to them. The son was Ganesha with an elephant head and human torso.

The other story is more popular. In it Parvati created Ganesha out of dirt from her body, when Shiva was not home, and asked Ganesha to be her bodyguard. Obedient to his mother, he sat outside the main door, while Parvati took a bath. Meanwhile Shiva returned home and faced Ganesha, who would not let him enter the house. The two did not know they were father and son, and a fight ensued in which Ganesha's head was cut off by Shiva. When Parvati came out, she was enraged to see her son beheaded, and Shiva, upset when he learned the whole story, asked her pardon,

21

promising to replace Ganesha's head. He brought a baby elephant's head and attached it to Ganesha's body with a new life.

Ganesha is said to have two wives: Siddhi and Buddhi, meaning "success" and "intellect." In a Ganesha *puja,* the worship of Siddhi and Buddhi is jointly performed because the worshipper needs success and intelligence in order to achieve his or her objective without any obstacle. Ganesha's vehicle is a mouse.

Ganesha has several other names such as *Ganapati* "troop lord," *Vinayaka* "Supreme leader," etc. One of his names is *Lambodara* "large bellied," which symbolizes the big womb in which resides the whole universe. Also, Ganesha loves to eat large, round, sweet confections called *modaka,* the *prasada* or sacramental food for his *puja.* Another name for Ganesha is *Ekadanta* "one tusker." In one story, he lost the second tusk in a fight with Parashu Rama. In another version he lost it in battle helping his brother Skanda, another great war hero. In still another story, Ganesha agreed to be the scribe for the epic *Mahabharata* on the request of its author Vyasa. Ganesha used the other tusk for a pen with which he wrote down the epic as dictated by Vyasa.

A Puranic story relates that Ganesha became the first god to be honored in any *puja.* Brahma, the Creator, was assigned the task of deciding which god should be given the honor of being worshipped first. He told the gods that whoever finished the race around the universe first would receive this honor. Since Ganesha's vehicle was a mouse he instead went quickly around his parents, Parvati and Shiva. Others, with faster vehicles, went around the universe, taking too long. When Ganesha told Brahma that the universe was the embodiment of Parvati and Shiva, Brahma declared that Ganesha had won the race. Hence, when starting any worthy project or work the name of Ganesha is remembered first. His famous mantra is:

Śrīganeśāya namah
Salutation to Lord Ganesha

The more interesting symbolism comes from the definition of Ganesha's name as "leader of the attendants or community." The attendants in mythology are Ganesha's troops, but in the *puja,* those participating are the troops led by Ganesha: the attendants are the worshipper, his or her family, and the community.

On the fourth day of the bright fortnight of the sixth Hindu month (*Bhadrapada* in August-September), Ganesha is worshipped as the central deity also. The festival is called *Ganesha Chaturthi* "Ganesha's fourth day."

GAURI:

The goddess Gauri is more popularly known as Parvati, spouse of Shiva. She is the daughter of Mena and Himavat. Her father's name, Himavat, has the same derivation as the Himalayas, the mountains that are called *Parvata;* hence the name *Parvati* or "Parvata's daughter." Her abode is the mountain Kailasa in the Himalayas. She uses a lion as her vehicle. Skanda as well as Ganesha is her son.

For Skanda's birth there are special stories. Parvati in her past life was called *Sati.* Her father was Daksha, himself a Prajapati. After Shiva married Sati, Daksha once performed a great *yajna* to which Shiva was not invited, and because of this insult, Sati threw herself in the fire-pit of the *yajna* and burned to death. Note that the word *sati* has been used for a widow who burns herself to death. When Shiva learned of his wife's death, he destroyed the entire *yajna* of Daksha.

In Sati's next birth as Parvati, she wanted to marry Shiva. But he had become a total ascetic after her death and was not interested in marriage. But the gods knew that only Shiva's son could kill the demons who had created havoc in the world and so they favored Parvati's marriage to Shiva. They encouraged her to win Shiva's favor with the help of Kama Deva, the god of love; Shiva burned Kama to show his displeasure. But Parvati did a great penance to please the ascetic Shiva, and finally they were married. Their son, Skanda later vanquished those demons, and the *Skanda Purana* is named after him.

In addition to Sati and Parvati, the goddess has thousands of names and forms. Philosophically she is Uma, who produces, sustains, and dissolves the universe. The cosmic cycle starts again and again with her power. She is, therefore, the mother of Cosmic Time or *Kali.* When she is calm she is known as *Gauri* "the white goddess." But in her active and aggressive form she is known as *Kali* "the black goddess," with thousands of weapons in her hands. She has killed demons such as Mahisha "buffalo" who created general havoc. The name signifying her power is *Shakti* "power," "energy," "force." Because of this name, her devotee may be called a *Shakta.* The

Shaktas worship Shakti in both tantric and non-tantric ways. A tantric *puja* follows procedures based on the tantra books, or *Agamas*. Shakti's tantric *pujas* include her spouse, Shiva. These *pujas* are full of mystical formulas, positions, gestures, diagrams and objects.

But in this Worship she is Gauri or the white goddess, obviously indicating that she is not to be worshipped with tantric formulas. In her Gauri form, she is seen by the *bhakta* or devotee as calm and pleased, like his mother, or *Amba*. After all Gauri is Mother Goddess, who cares for her child, the devotee. Yet she is also *Durga* "the incomprehensible," which makes her challenging for the seeker. Her devotees, in awe of her mystery, attempt to reach her emotionally with loud praises such as:

Jaya Durge!
Victory (to you), Durga!

Durga's most popular independent *puja* in which she is the central deity falls between the seventh and tenth day of the bright fortnight of the seventh month (*Ashvina* or September-October). It is known as the *Durga Puja*.

SHIVA

The Hindu cycle of creation, preservation, and destruction is represented by three gods: Brahma, Vishnu, and Shiva. But the meaning of Shiva is "good" or "happy." Thus Shiva's destruction is meant only for good. The other name of Shiva is *Rudra* "fierce," which symbolizes the destructive aspect. His cosmic dance to destroy the aged universe is known as the *tandava*. He opens a third eye, between his eyebrows, and from there emanates the destructive fire. Because dance causes cosmic dissolution, he is called *Nataraja* "the dance lord." It is told that once Shiva burned Kama (the love god) with the fire from his third eye. But Rati, the wife of Kama, prayed to the compassionate lord and he revived Kama in abstract form.

Shiva is in human form and wears only a lower garment, which is a tigerskin. He is smeared with ashes. Although he is everywhere, his real abode is Kailasa, the mountain, which symbolizes highest divinity. He has four arms and holds a drum in his hand. His weapon is generally a trident. Over his head is a crescent moon and the river Ganges is held on his head, from which it flows onto the earth below. A cobra is around his neck. His vehicle is a bull called *Nandin* "the delightful." In pictures of other iconographic representations, Shiva is shown with his wife, Parvati, and the two sons, Skanda and Ganesha.

In his non-iconic form, Shiva is shown as a *linga,* which means "symbol" or "sign." In mythology the *linga* appears as an ithyphallic symbol, suggesting that the cosmos emerges from it. Thus Shiva is not only the dissolver but the creator of the entire cosmos. He is the preserver also. For example, because he drank the cosmic poison that came from the churning of the cosmic ocean, all life was saved. Since the poison was so deadly that it left a blue mark on Shiva's throat, he is called also the Blue Throat or *Nilakantha.*

The yogis consider Shiva their lord; hence his name *Yogishvara* (*yogi* "a yoga practitioner" and *ishvara* "lord"). Most popular in yoga for meditation is the five-syllable mantra *namah Sivaya* (*namah* "salutation" and *Sivāya* "to Shiva"). According to the Shaivas, the devotees or worshippers of Shiva, this mantra is good for everyone, irrespective of race, rank, region, and religion. It requires no guru (spiritual teacher) for initiation and has no restrictions of any sort.

Shiva is called *Ardhanarishvara* (*ardha* "half," *nari* "woman," "lady," and *ishvara* "lord"), meaning that Shiva is half-female and half-male. This concept symbolizes oneness or the union of Shiva and Shakti, a popular symbolism, especially in tantric ritualism. In actual belief, this is the union of good and power. Good must be pursued with power, and power should be used for good. Without Shakti or power, Shiva (good) is *Shava,* which means "corpse," or "dead." In one story Parvati assumes her *Chandi* or "terror" form to kill demons. In the rage of killing demons, there was a confusion, which caused her to kill Shiva also. When she resumed her calm form, she revived Shiva, and the two were in happy union once more. Shiva "the good" can be confused with demons "the bad" when Chandi "the indiscriminate power" is used to eliminate the bad.

The Worship emphasizes the family life as its main objective. In the Worship, therefore, the worshipper invites Gauri, "the calm and compassionate" and Shiva, the "good and auspicious," led by their child Ganesha, the obstacle remover.

Shiva's independent *puja* is held on several occasions; the most popular is the *Shiva-ratri* or Shiva's Night, the fourteenth day of the dark fortnight of the last Hindu month (*Phalguna* or February-March).

SURYA

Surya is the sun god. His other and more important name is *Savitr* or *Savitar*, "impeller," or "the sun." Prayer to him is recommended daily, as he comes and goes every day from east to west.

The best times for daily prayers are sunrise, noon, and sunset, which are believed to be the junctions or *sandhi* of the day; hence prayer at these times is called *sandhya* or "junctional prayer." Since these are good times for meditation, the mantras suitable for meditation make up the *sandhya*. The most famous *sandhya* mantra found in the *Rig Veda* is *gayatri* or "singer-savior," named after its meter, which is called *gayatri*. But to differentiate it from other prayers in this meter it is called *Savitri*, the prayer for *Savitr*. It is dedicated to the Sun as follows:

> We meditate on that desirable
> radiance of the Divine Impeller.
> May he activate our intellects.

One of the names of Surya is *Vivasvat* "vivifier" or "radiator." According to Puranic tradition, Vivasvat is the son of Kashyapa and Aditi. After his mother, he is called Aditya, and his brothers are Adityas (e.g., the eight famous Aditya brothers). Kashyapa, his father, is a Prajapati, or first progenitor of beings. Vivasvat's wife is Samjna "consciousness." She gave birth to two sons and a daughter, who are Manu, Yama, and Yami. Yumuna, the sacred river from the Himalayas, is Yami.

For Samjna it became too difficult to endure the heat of Vivasvat. She left home, leaving her own shadow or *Chhaya* as the caretaker of her children. Vivasvat mistook Chhaya for Samjna and took her as his wife. They had two sons and one daughter, namely, Savarni, Shani, and Tapati. Shani means "slow mover," which is the planet Saturn, son of the Sun.

Later Vivasvat met his wife Samjna who was in the disguise of a mare. They had two more sons, the famous Ashvin ("horse's son") twins, known also as the first physicians.

Surya and his family symbolize important aspects of life. He is associated with Samjna, which we have seen means "consciousness." Human beings are called *manava* or "Manu's children"; Manu, the original ancestor of the human race, is Surya's son. His own son, Yama, is the god of death. His daughter Yamuna is known as a river and a mother who replenishes life with her waters. The Ashvin twins, Nasatya and Dasra, symbolize healing. Surya is worshipped also with other planets as their head. He is also called *Surya Narayana* "Surya as Narayana," thus identifying him with Vishnu, the preserver.

THE SPATIAL DEITIES

The concept of space is very complex in the Puranic mythology. Space is called "loka." The most common belief is that Brahma, the four-headed Creator born on a lotus from Vishnu's navel, created *loka,* which means "world" also. There are four main directions: south, north, east, and west, and four intermediate directions–thus eight directions in the context of this *puja.*

Since by tradition each direction needs to be guarded or protected, there are eight guardians or protectors. A world guardian is called *Lokapala* "space protector." There are various names for each *Lokapala,* and there sometimes is Vedic and Puranic fusion between their personalties. For example, Soma is the planet Moon in the Puranic mythology. But the mantra for the Moon, like for other *Lokapalas,* is Vedic which, is in praise of Soma, the intoxicating drink of the Vedic Aryans. The drink became extinct long before the Puranic literature started, but in the Puranic *pujas* and mythology, Moon possesses this drink as nectar or ambrosia. Below is a brief description of the *Lokapalas.*

(1) **Yama:** He is the *Lokapala* or guardian of the south. As god of death he judges all dead persons as to the kind of next life they will get, according to their karmas or deeds.

(2) **Soma:** The northern zone is ruled by Soma, who is Moon. He came out of the churning of the cosmic sea, which is described elsewhere.

(3) **Indra:** As the celebrated Vedic god, he is the king of gods. He is the *Lokapala* of the eastern zone. In later mythology he controls rains.

(4) **Varuna:** Another famous Vedic god who originally watched the universal order or regulation called *rita* in the Vedas. Later he became the lord of waters and is worshipped in a water jar or vessel. Brahma made him the *Lokapala* for the western quarter.

(5) **Nirriti**: The goddess Nirriti was born of the cosmic sea when it was churned by the gods and demons together. She is also called *Jyeshtha* "the elder," as she is the older sister of Lakshmi, the goddess of prosperity. Nirriti, as the goddess of sins, is worshipped by the demons. Being an elder goddess she has been appointed as a *Lokapala* for the intermediate direction of southwest.

(6) **Vayu**: This is the Vedic god of "wind" (*Vayu* "wind" or "air"). He was appointed *Lokapala* for the intermediate direction of northwest.

(7) **Ishana**: This god is identified with Rudra or Shiva. He is *Lokapala* for the intermediate direction of northeast.

(8) **Agni**: This god's name means "fire." He is the most important god, as all oblations are carried to other gods by him. The oblations will be discussed later. Agni is *Lokapala* for the intermediate direction of southeast.

In later mythology, Kubera, a very important god who is the custodian of all the wealth of the world, was appointed another *Lokapala* in the north.

There are several reasons for the zonal or spatial assignments of deities. As discussed before, a mystical reason is the mandala. But there is another mandala concept involved here. Brahma, the Creator god who has four heads, sits in the center of the mandala space. With his four heads he watches all the directions of his creation. The *Lokapalas* help Brahma, by guarding his *lokas* or worlds. The directions represent the seats of the *Lokapalas* in the mandala. The worshipper wants favors from all the directions of his world for the success of his wish.

There may be historical reasons also. For example, Yama is god of death and rules the south. The early Aryans, while moving southward in the subcontinent always faced the possibility of death in their battles with the Dravidians.

THE NINE PLANETARY GODS

The Worship includes the honoring of the *nava grahas* (*nava* "nine", *graha* "planet"). All nine male deities are introduced below in the order of their offerings in the *puja*.

(1) **Surya**: The Sun, the central planet among all others.

(2) **Chandra**: The word Chandra means "shiny." He is the Moon, and his other popular name is *Soma*.

(3) **Bhauma**: The meaning of *Bhauma* is "son of earth" (from *bhu* "earth"). The most common name for him is *Mangala* "auspicious," the same as the planet Mars.

(4) **Budha**: This is Mercury. His name means "intelligent." He is the son of Soma, hence called *Saumya* or "gentle."

(5) **Brihaspati**: This is Jupiter, the guru or teacher of the gods, hence his name, which means "the big master" or the *Guru*.

(6) **Shukra**: He refers to Venus but is a male. His name means "bright," and he is believed to be the teacher of demons.

(7) **Shani**: This is Saturn, son of Surya.

These seven planetary names correspond to the days of the week in the order of Sunday to Saturday. The following two are considered the "shadowy" planets or nodes.

(8) **Rahu**: His name means "grabber." He is the mythical demon who grabs or eclipses the Moon. In the disguise of a god he received ambrosia (*amrita* or "immortalizer") from Vishnu who was in the instant form or avatar of a beautiful woman named *Mohini* "the enchantress." Rahu was exposed by the Sun and the Moon, and Vishnu beheaded him instantly, but his head and torso remained alive, because the ambrosia had already immortalized his entire body. Since then, Rahu's head eclipses the Moon in revenge.

(9) **Ketu**: This is the torso of Rahu and eclipses the Sun.

The positions of the nine *grahas* are shown in a person's horoscope. Every traditional Hindu, if success in life is needed quickly, is required to propitiate the planets according to his or her horoscope. The basis for the belief in astrology is that the planets affect our behavior and activities. Symbolically, this planet worship represents human respect for the environment.

NARAYANA

With Narayana are associated several meanings, some justified linguistically and others philosophically and mythologically. The compound term is made of two simple words: *nara* and *ayana*. Underlying *nara* is the word *nara* or "man," thus giving *nara* its meaning "of man," "from man," "manly," "human." The word *ayana* means "abode," "place," or "residence," and thus Narayana is "human abode." In a philosophical sense every human body is pervaded by Narayana, who is Vishnu. The meaning of Vishnu is "Pervader."

Some scholars, such as Manu, author of the law book, *Manusmriti,* interprets Narayana as formed from two words, *nara* and *ayana.* He considers *nārā* (rather than *nara)* as the basic word which, according to him, means "waters." In mythology, Lord Narayana's ultimate residence is in the waters that symbolize evolution as well as dissolution of life. Lord Narayana made Brahma, the Creator, on a lotus, out of his navel. Brahma could not find the source of this lotus. Narayana rests in these cosmic waters on a cosmic serpent named Shesha "the remainder" or Ananta "the endless."

In *bhakti* literature, Narayana symbolizes the beginning, the middle, and the end of all, even though Narayana is beyond everything. Thus he is within and without, at once immanent and transcendental. He is formless, yet assumes form or avatar in order to rescue his devotees and the world. Not only Brahma, the Creator, but Shiva, the Destroyer, are his forms. Thus he is ultimately one and everything: creator, sustainer, and destroyer of everything. To know him as the Supreme Being in oneself is the true knowledge, because he is the Truth or *Satya.* This knowledge, following the path of bhakti, gives the *bhakta* final liberation or *mukti.*

In the Story his name is Satya Narayana, the same as Vishnu whose spouse is the beautiful Lakshmi. He is usually worshipped with Lakshmi as she is the goddess of prosperity. The goal of the Satya Narayana *puja* is prosperity for the worshipper. In this *puja,* Vishnu is invited as the main deity and guest. He comes to the *puja* from his residence called *Vaikuntha* "the state or place beyond sorrow." He comes as quickly as possible, riding on his fast-flying vehicle Garuda "eagle"; hence his name is *Garudadhvaja,* whose *dhvaja* "banner" or "mover" is *Garuda.*

In the Worship, those participating meditate on Vishnu at the time of invocation. For easy meditation he is visualized in his human-type form, which has the following features: four arms holding a conch, a disc, a mace, and a lotus. These are the symbols of creation (conch and lotus), protection, and destruction (disc and mace). He has a garland of wild flowers around his neck, and on his chest is a special curl of hair called *shrivatsa.*

The Story says that Narada, the sage who is his oldest ideal devotee, saw Narayana in this human-type form, so he is worshipped with an image that has human features. But Narayana's most popular non-iconic symbol is a stone called *shalagrama* (also *shaligrama).* This stone is a rounded ammonite fossil found in the Gandak river in Nepal and India.

There are many small and big temples dedicated to Narayana or Vishnu. Among the most revered temples are at Badrinath in the Himalayas in the north, Rameshwaram in the south, Puri in the east and Dwaraka in the west. Another very sacred temple mentioned in the Story is Ranganatha, from *ranga* "play," "fun," "joy," "pleasure" and *natha* "Lord." Today, this temple's place is known in southern India as Srirangam.

A temple of the Lord is not only a place of worship, but also a symbol of his *vishva* meaning "All." In the Worship a verse says that the Lord has spread out this *vishva* or cosmos by or for his *lila* "sport," "game," "play," "fun." The devotee wants to enjoy Lord's creation. This is why *pujas,* including the present one, whether in a temple or a house, are frequently accompanied by devotional music and dance. The whole ritual is a play to entertain God.

THE AVATARAS

Avatar or *avatara* means descent or descending down (*ava* "down," *tara* "crossing over" or "passing across"). This concept basically means the coming down of a person who saves us (as from a sea) by getting us "across." For this purpose a deity assumes any form, which can be called the "avatara" form. There are avatars of the various deities, but the clear conceptualization of avatar appears in the *Bhagavad Gita.*

There Krishna tells his friend Arjuna in a verse:

> Whenever there is fall of dharma, O Arjuna!
> And rise of non-dharma, then I create myself.
> To protect the gentle, to destroy the evil doers,
> And to establish dharma I appear in age after age.

Thus, loss of *dharma* or duty, righteousness, norm, virtue, law, fairness, right conduct, etc., prompts God to appear as savior or avatar. Here Krishna is God, i.e., Vishnu's avatar. The meaning of Vishnu is generally given as "Pervader" as this word is derived from the verb *vish* "to enter, pervade." From a philosophical point of view Vishnu means "who has entered everything" as well as "into whom everything enters." With this interpretation, as said earlier, all forms are Vishnu or Narayana.

Vishnu's famous ten avatars are: Fish (*Matsya*), Tortoise (*Kurma*), Boar (*Varaha*), Man-Lion (*Narasimha*), Dwarf (*Vamana*), Parashu Rama, Rama, Bala Rama, Krishna, and Buddha.

In the fish avatar Vishnu saved Manu, the father of human beings, from drowning in the "big flood." He became a tortoise to hold on his back the mountain Mandara for further churning of the cosmic ocean. As a boar, Vishnu kept the earth up in his tusks, thus saving her (Earth is a female deity) from drowning. He became half-man and half-lion in order to kill Hiranyakashipu, who was trying to burn his own son, Prahlada, a great devotee of Vishnu. In order to drive the demon king Bali out, Vishnu became a dwarf man and took three giant steps to cover the earth and heaven, which Bali was forced to leave for the underworld.

Then there are five avatars in which Vishnu has normal human forms. He was born as a Brahmin. His weapon was an axe (*parashu*), hence he is called Parashu Rama, or the "Rama with the axe." During this avatar he destroyed several bad Kshatriya kings.

His avatar as Rama, son of Ayodhya's king Dasharatha, is the hero of the epic *Ramayana*. Now as Kshatriya avatar, Rama killed the demon king Ravana who had abducted Sita, i.e., Rama's wife.

Vishnu then is born as two brothers: Bala Rama the older, and Krishna the younger, in order to destroy Kamsa, the cruel king of Mathura.

Vishnu is born also as Buddha to oppose several Vedic practices and beliefs, such as animal sacrifice.

Inclusion of Buddha here implies that the avatar person does not necessarily accept or agree with other religions, including his or her own ancestor's. In this respect Moses, Zoroaster, Christ, Muhammad, and many others outside the Hindu tradition would be considered as "saviors," which essentially is equivalent to the meaning of the term, *avatar*. The view that God has several names and representatives is quite popular. For example, I personally recorded a Hindu folk ritual in the foothills of the Central Himalayas in which Muhammad was identified with Vishnu. The following Hindi bhajan (devotional song), a favorite of Mahatma Gandhi, is often sung in praise of Satya Narayana toward the end of his *puja:*

Īshwar allāh tere nām
Sab ko sanmati de bhagwān
Ishvara and Allah are your names,
To all give guidance, O God!

Another major avatar with the name Kalkin is to be born in *Kali yuga*, the fourth and the last age of our earth.

The Satya Narayana is identified in the Worship with the Man-Lion, Rama, Krishna, etc. For example, *Janaki-Vallabha* "Sita's beloved" is Rama. Similarly *Gokulananda* "Gokula's joy," *Govinda* "herdsman," "cowfinder," "body protector," etc., all refer to Krishna, who lived in the village of Gokula, near Mathura, with his foster parents, Nanda and Yashoda. Krishna's other name, *Vāsudeva,* is also mentioned; his real father was Vasudeva and his real mother was Devaki. They were imprisoned by Kamsa, the cruel king of Mathura because of the prophecy that Kamsa would be slain by their son, and all of their children were killed by Kamsa. But Krishna, just after his birth, was secretly taken away to Nanda and Yashoda, and later slew Kamsa. This is why Narayana, destroyer of Kamsa and other evil-doers, is called *Daityasudana* "Demon slayer" in the Worship.

The Story also has clear examples of instant avatars. For instance, Narayana appears as a Brahmin to instruct the poor Brahmin how to perform this *puja*. In another story, Narayana, in the disguise of a monk, meets the merchant and his son-in-law. The monk is called *Dandin* "stick holder." The term is a pun in the Story, meaning "monk" as well as "punisher," "police officer," and *danda* "staff," "a stick," or "club" is the symbol of a law-enforcement officer as well as of a monk. The avatar person is expected to do justice or enforce law and order–i.e., *dharma*. Like a king, the avatar also follows the four *upayas* or means of enforcing law and order. These are: *saman* "settlement," "peace," "conciliation," *dana* "donation," "favor," *bheda* "break-up," "tearing," and *danda* "punishment."

In all episodes of the Story we observe that the instant avatars resort to one or more of these means in the order of peaceful negotiation (*saman),* granting favors (*dana),* creating problems (*bheda)* and punishment (*danda).* A regular avatar such as Rama followed a similar pattern with Ravana. He wanted peace with Ravana through mutual favors. When the first two means were ignored by Ravana, Rama created more and more difficulties and eventually punished Ravana on the battlefield by death.

It should be noted that Narayana is invited to the *puja* place where the "life establishment" ritual is performed as if a fresh avatar to help the worshipper is taking place then and there. The Vedic offerings that are used to worship Narayana are from the *Purusha* hymn of the *Rig Veda*. The Purusha or "Proto-Being" is also considered the first avatar of Narayana, hence called the *Adi Purusha* or "First Person."

All avatars mentioned thus far are male, but avatars can be male or female. A famous female avatar of Vishnu is Mohini, "the Enchantress." She is related to Vishnu's tortoise avatar that occurred during the churning of the cosmic sea. The story is as follows:

Advised by Brahma and Vishnu, the gods and demons began to churn the cosmic sea, their main objective being to obtain a drink called *amrita* or "immortalizer," since they all wanted to become immortal. The Mandara mountain was used as the churning rod. Vasuki, a cosmic serpent, became the rope whose tail was pulled by the gods and his head by the demons. Herbs growing on the Mandara mountain were dumped into the sea for churning. During the churning, the mountain became unstable. At that time Vishnu became a tortoise who held the mountain on his shell.

Some miraculous beings and objects came out of this cosmic churning. One was Nirriti, the goddess of sins. Her younger sister was Lakshmi, the goddess of grace, beauty, and prosperity. Lakshmi chose Vishnu, the most handsome male. The deadliest poison, *Kalakuta,* came also out of the sea; Shiva drank it all. Other products include a horse, a cow, an elephant, a gem, a tree and the moon. The gem is called *Kaustubha* and was presented to Vishnu. Then came Dhanvantari, the god of medical science, with a pot or *kumbha* full of *amrita* or ambrosia, the immortalizing drink.

The gods did not want the demons to share the drink. So Vishnu became a charming woman called Mohini whose beauty enchanted all the demons. However, one demon named Rahu joined the gods in disguise when Mohini was distributing the drink to the gods only. Rahu drank it but, when exposed by other gods, was beheaded instantly. His head and torso, however, remained immortal. When the demons, who were under the spell of Mohini, woke up and found the drink was gone, they quarreled and fought with the gods who, aided by Vishnu, vanquished all the demons.

For the *puja* the important person and object are Lakshmi and the *kumbha*. Lakshmi is automatically identified with Narayana. The *kumbha* is represented in the *puja* by a vessel called *Kalasha*.

THE NARRATORS AND THE LISTENERS

The main narrators and listeners of the Worship and the Story include these persons: Vyasa, Suta, Shaunaka and Narada, all famous names in Indian literature. A traditional or mythological introduction of these names follows.

(1) **Vyasa:** He is the traditional author or editor of many great books including the Puranas. He arranged the *Vedas,* authored the *Vedanta Sutras*, and the great epic, the *Mahabharata.* To give a unifying touch to these classics, the tradition coined the name of a common author. The tradition of anonymity in authorship has been continuous, with authors writing under the name of a famous person with whose tradition they identified. Some hold that this tradition developed from humility on the part of these anonymous writers who were said to be more interested in propagation or preservation of the literature than in perpetuation of their names.

Nevertheless, the Hindu tradition believes that there was indeed one Vyasa whose hermitage or *ashrama* was near the present-day Badrinath in the Central Himalayas. His mother was a fisherwoman named Satyavati, and his father Parashara. Sage Parashara left Satyavati on an island when she was pregnant. Vyasa was born on this island or *dvipa* and was named Krishna Dvaipayana, or the Krishna from the Dvipa. Thus he is not confused with the other Krishna, son of Vasudeva and Devaki. Other names of Vyasa include Badarayana, Satyavatisuta, and Parasharya. In the Hindu view, Vyasa is the greatest teacher in the world. So *guru puja* or "teacher worship" is synonymous with *Vyasa Puja*, a popular Hindu way to honor the profession of teaching.

(2) **Suta:** The name Suta in Puranic literature is associated with the main storyteller. Suta's father was Romaharshana. Vyasa told all the stories to Suta. In our Story also, Suta addresses the eighty-eight thousand *rishis* or sages headed by Shaunaka, another sage. The Story is retold by Suta in Naimisha, a sacred forest in the northern plains of India.

Suta, like Vyasa, seems to be a common name for any great storyteller in the Puranas, and several authors have added their stories to the Puranas at various times under the generic name *Suta*. With this name the stories such as the Satya Narayana's became popular among the masses.

(3) **Shaunaka**: The name *Shaunaka* is associated with several important works such as *Shaunakasmriti, Brihaddevata,* etc. The tradition says that the sole author of such works is Shaunaka, whose father was Shaunahotra, a friend of the god, Indra. The motive for the use of this name in popular literature seems to be the same as in the case of Vyasa and Suta.

(4) **Narada**: Narada's name is associated with various works in the same manner as that of Vyasa and Suta. According to one myth, Brahma, the Creator, produced Narada out of his head. So Narada is Brahma's brainchild, hence called *Devarshi* or "the divine seer." He received a *vina,* a musical string instrument, from his father Brahma, and with this instrument, sings devotional songs in praise of Vishnu. One of his functions is to receive news and give it to others in the interest of greater good. Mythologically, therefore, Narada is the first journalist. He moves from one world to another. In the Story he goes to Vaikuntha, the world of Vishnu, to seek an easy method for achieving human happiness. The Story and the Worship are the answers that Narada received from Vishnu.

Above all, Narada is known to be the greatest expounder of devotional love or *bhakti,* especially Vaishnava devotionalism. Many devotional works are accredited to him, including *Naradapancharatra, Naradasmriti, Naradagita, Naradasamhita, Naradapurana,* etc. The most popular work on the concept of *bhakti,* the *Naradabhaktisutra,* bears his name also. This work contains *bhakti* formulas or aphorisms (*sutra*) that are quoted frequently as authoritative statements on various aspects of devotion.

BHAKTI

Two ancient authorities on the philosophy of *bhakti* are Narada and Shandilya. Narada defines *bhakti* as the highest form of love for the deity. Shandilya considers it as super attachment to Godhead.

No Hindu religious concept can claim more impact on Indian culture than the concept of *bhakti.* There are several opinions on its basic nature. Of the three major paths to salvation, *bhakti* is considered the easiest, hence popular among the common folk. The other two paths are knowledge (*jnana*) and action (*karma*). The Sanskrit word *bhakti* means many things. Its common dictionary meanings include: sharing, division, partition, distribution, and devotion, among others. These meanings are all helpful in understanding the philosophy and practice of the concept.

An important devotional aspect of *bhakti* is its advocacy of a personal relationship between the devotee and the deity. It is not so important who the deity is. One could choose Vishnu, Shiva, Devi, or others, as a personal deity. It is necessary, however, that the deity be conceived as a person, with or without a body or form. From this point of view, *bhakti* is divided into two basic approaches: devotees who believe that Godhead has no form or qualities are classified as the followers of the *nirguna bhakti*. The term *nirguna* is compounded of *nir* "non" and *guna* "quality." Those who believe that Godhead basically is *nirguna,* but can at will appear with form are devotees of the *saguna* school. *Saguna* means "with quality."

A form is a natural expression. Nature or *Prakriti* is characterized by *gunas* or qualities. *Guna* means "rope," "loop," "strand," even though the frequent translation is "quality," or "form." A form is evolved by the combination of three gunas; namely, *sattva, rajas,* and *tamas.* *Sattva* generally means "good," symbolizing light, calm, sublime, brilliant, and compassionate quality; the *rajas* suggests dusty, active, energetic, and passionate quality; the *tamas* stands for "bad" quality, dark, dirty, lazy, violent, stupid, etc. Every form or being develops differently, because the combination of these three strands or *gunas* in each is different.

In the Worship Narayana is called *Gunatita* "outside gunas," yet with *gunatraya* "the guna-triad, or the combination of the three gunas." This paradox corresponds to the Story, in which it is stated that Lord Narayana has no form, beginning, middle, or end. But Narada sees him in the human form and they talk like two humans discussing how to help fellow humans. It is Vishnu's grace that he assumes a form that a bhakta or devotee such as Narada can identify closely with.

Clearly *bhakti* is based on the principle of dualism known as *dvaita.* In simpler terms, there is God on the one hand and His creation on the other. In this respect *bhakti* as a principle is common, not only to most Indian religions, but also to such other major religions as Judaism, Christianity, and Islam.

In opposition to the dualistic view of *bhakti* there is the Vedanta outlook, based on non-dualism and called *advaita* (*a* "non" and *dvaita* "duality"), which espouses the belief that the single Universal Self or Brahman alone is true; the rest is false. The plurality of beings and things appears to us because of ignorance (*ajnana*) or illusion known as *maya.*

Knowledge is the means of removing this illusion, which originates from
Brahman itself. Put simply, the duality of God and creation disappears with
true knowledge, which means liberation.

The *bhakti* followers aim also for liberation and believe that the easier
path is the "*bhakti* way" (*bhakti marga*) rather than the knowledge way
(*jnana marga*). It is not that they do not recognize the power and value of
knowledge. They believe that *bhakti* eventually can yield knowledge coming
from God's grace.

The *bhakti* way, according to Narada, is experienced in eleven kinds
of relationships that a devotee can establish with the deity. Among these,
four are noteworthy: service (*dasya*), spousal love (*kanta*), friendship
(*sakhya*) and parental affection (*vatsalya*). In the service relationship, the
deity is the boss and the devotee is the servant. The Worship and the Story
emphasize this relationship. The love relationship is exemplified by the love
of Radha for Krishna. Radha was a young beautiful milkmaid, and Krishna,
the young handsome cowboy of Vraja. The other young cowboys of Vraja
loved Krishna as their best friend. The affection relationship is expressed
by Yashoda, foster mother of Krishna; here Yashoda, the devotee, selflessly
looks after the Lord who is subordinated to her as her son.

The Bhagavata Purana's "nine-means" *bhakti* system is often considered
to be the standard in the Vaishnava faith. These nine are: hearing about
Vishnu (*shravana*), singing about him (*kirtana*), remembering him
(*smarana*), serving his feet (*pada-sevana* "feet-serving"), worshipping
(*archana*), bowing to him (*vandana*), servicing him (*dasya*), befriending him
(*sakhya*), and self-submitting to him (*atma-nivedana* "self-presenting").

A devotee is free to choose any relationship and God will make
Himself available through that relationship. This is what God as Krishna in
the *Gita* says:

> Whoever follow me by whatever way,
> I share with them by that very one.

The verb "share" is only one translation of the Sanskrit verb *bhaj*, which
occurs in the verse (as *bhajami* "I share, devote, serve, present, submit,
grant favor, dedicate, etc."). The words *bhakti* "devotion," *bhakta*
"devotee," and *Bhagavan* "God" are derived from this verb. More of *bhakti*

will be discussed later to emphasize the point that the Satya Narayana ritual performance is essentially a *bhakti* way.

TIME AND CREATION

In the Story we are told that the proposed Worship is the shortest and easiest solution for achieving happiness in the Age of Kali. The concept of "ages" is related to the Puranic notion of time in the context of Brahma and his creation. It is briefly discussed below.

In the popular Hindu view, all things and beings and the universe also experience the cycle of creation, preservation, and dissolution through time. Three deities—Brahma, Vishnu, and Shiva—represent the three phases of this cycle.

Brahma is assigned the task of creating *srishti* or *samsara* "creation, world, universe," meaning literally "that which moves or flows forward all around." Brahma's four heads and four hands symbolize the power of such movement. He rides on a white swan symbolizing movement and enlightenment. The Vedas in one of his hands symbolize the knowledge that he gave to humans. The Vedic *Prajapati* or "Progenitor" is later identified as Brahma. But the stories about the origin of Prajapati and Brahma in the Vedic and post-Vedic mythologies are not identical. Two popular Puranic stories are given below.

According to one story, Brahma was born of an egg that developed from cosmic waters full of creative elements. This egg of Brahma *Brahmanda* (*Brahma* "Creator" and *anda* "egg") contains inside of it all the great evolutionary plan. It is also called the *hiranyagarbha* or "golden womb." After Brahma is born of this womb he produces many objects or beings from his body.

In another story, Brahma was produced on a lotus that grew out of Vishnu's navel. It is Vishnu who rests on *Ananta* or "Infinite," symbolized as a cosmic serpent named *Shesha*, or "Remainder." Vishnu lying over Shesha resides in the Milky Sea called *Kshira Sagara* (*kshira* "milk," *sagara* "sea"). Brahma attempted to find the roots of the lotus from which he came. He looked all around, thus developing four heads, but failed to locate the roots.

Finally, he started creation from his own body. As the oldest father, he is called the Grandfather *(Pitamaha),* and there is a long list of what he produced. Among his first "mental" *(manasa)* sons are Marichi, Angiras, Atri, Pulastya, Pulaha and Kratu. Beside these first sages are his other famous sons, the four sages Sanaka, Sananda, Sanatana, and Sanatkumara. In our Story, Narada too is his son.

Then Brahma created from his body a goddess called Sarasvati who, being the first woman, became his wife. She is shown with a stringed instrument called *vina* and a book representing her as the goddess of music and learning. Her vehicle is a white swan. Her independent worship is called *Sarasvati Puja.* But there is no such independent *puja* for her father, Brahma, since he took her as his wife—disrespectable and, hence, unacceptable social conduct, being incestuous. His later creation includes Manu from his body's right side and Shatarupa "the woman with hundreds of forms" from the left side. The two children became husband and wife. Manu is the first father of man; hence, humans are called after him *manavas.*

Brahmic creation involves the Puranic notion of Brahmic time, explained mainly in *yugas* and *manvantaras*—two different systems, briefly described below:

The term *yuga* means "age," or "epoch." There are four *yugas:* *Satya, Treta, Dvapara,* and *Kali.* Their respective time-ratios are 4:3:2:1. These four make a "mega-age" called *mahayuga,* consisting of 4,320,000 years. One world cycle equals a mega-age. One thousand mega-ages make a *kalpa.* There are 4,320,000,000 human years in one *kalpa,* which equals one day of Brahma.

The human year in the Hindu lunar calendar consists of twelve months. These are *Chaitra* (March-April), *Vaishakha* (April-May), *Jyeshtha* (May-June), *Ashadha* (June-July), *Shravana* (July-August), *Bhadrapada* (August-September), *Ashvina* (September-October), *Karttika* (October-November), *Agrahayana* (November-December), *Pausha* (December-January), *Magha* (January-February), *Phalguna* (February-March). Each month is divided into two lunar halves or fortnights—the bright and the dark. Each fortnight consists of fifteen days, thus making 360 days in one year. Another month is added every five years to adjust the lunar calendar to the solar calendar.

One day of a fortnight is called *tithi.* The *puja* days are referred to in terms of *tithis.* For example, the preferred day for the present puja is *paurnamasi* or the "full moon day," which completes the lunar month; the *Sarasvati Puja* is held on the fifth day of the bright fortnight of the eleventh month (January-February). The seven weekdays, based on the seven planets, as stated in the "nine planetary gods," are referred to also, but they are secondary to *tithis*.

The Brahmic day is divided also into fourteen *manvantaras* (*manu* and *antara*) meaning "Manu's intervals or periods." This is connected with the *yuga* division of time. Seventy-one mega-ages (*mahayugas*) make one *manvantara*. The current *manvantara* is called the *Vaivasvata*, as its ruler is Manu, the son of *Vivasvat* "Sun." It is believed that each *manvantara* has a different Manu. Six *manvantaras* have already passed. The Manu of the first *manvantara* was Svayambhuva "son of the self-born," as mentioned in the Story. The *kalpas* are associated with the *manvantaras*. The current *kalpa* or Brahmic day is called *shvetavaraha* or "white boar's."

When a Brahmic day is over, the creation is over also. The end is called *pralaya* "absorption," or "dissolution." During the Brahmic night, which equals the Brahmic day in length, Brahma rests; that is, he sleeps. When his night is over, he starts another cycle of creation. He lives for one hundred Brahmic years. The current Brahmic time is the first day of his fifty-first year. At the death of Brahma, there is *mahapralaya* "mega-dissolution." That is, the entire cosmos is absorbed or disappears into *Narayana*, who rests for one hundred Brahmic years and then produces another Brahma.

The cycle of appearance and disappearance of cosmos is Narayana's game or *lila* that he makes and unmakes with his power called *maya*. Due to his *maya, asat* the non-existent appears as *sat* existent. He alone has *sat*, hence, the name, Satya Narayana; he also has *cit* "consciousness" and *ananda* "bliss"; hence, he is also called *Sachchidananda* which is the same as the Vedantic Brahman. It is customary to state the current Brahmic time just before the worshipper takes the vow to worship Satya Narayana, whom not even Brahma knows.

From the point of view of *yuga* the best and full age is *Satya* as it is called also *Krita* "full, perfect, done." After the first age, i.e., the *Satya Yuga*, there is continuous decline of *dharma*. The worst age is the last one, the Kali. Metaphorically, *dharma* is considered as a cow who has four legs in the *Satya Yuga*, three legs in the *Treta*, two in the *Dvapara*, and only one in *Kali*.

Narayana assumes avatars in each *yuga:* e.g., he was Rama in *Treta* and Krishna in *Dvapara*. The first quarter of *Kali Yuga* has already seen the avatar of Buddha, as usually stated just before the "vow" of the *pujas*. The avatar to appear in the future is named as Kalkin; he will help stop the *dharma* from declining.

The followers of *bhakti* believe that it alone is the way to receive God's favor or grace in *Kali Yuga*. Even remembering God's "name" is enough to receive *mukti* or salvation. As the Sikh guru, Tegh Bahadur, says:

In *Kali Yuga* one attains *mukti* by God's name.

The Puranic *bhakti* religion is ritualistic. The story recommends the Worship or *vrata* of Satya Narayana as a "short solution" *(laghu upaya)* for the elimination of *Kali Yuga's* misery; God's name is included in the *puja* for remembering, singing, etc.

LIBERATION

The Story frequently mentions *moksha* or *mukti* and *muktas*. The words *moksha* or *mukti* mean "release, relief, salvation, liberation." *Mukti* is generally understood to take place at or after death. But one can achieve "live liberation," called *jivan-mukti*, and an individual who does is called *jivan-mukta* "the living liberated." *Moksha* is the ultimate among the traditional four goals of life. The other three are *dharma, artha,* and *kama*. These goals correspond to the cycle of personal growth from childhood to old age. The early life of the child is spent in learning the code or *dharma* of his or her social group, and it includes study also. Once the student life is over, one has to find a job for *artha* "earning" in order to have earthly or worldly gains. With earning, one can attend to household pleasures or *kama* "material desires." As retirement draws near, one should look for stress-free life or liberation, which is *moksha*.

Philosophically, however, *moksha* is related to freedom from life's misery here and hereafter; that is, from rebirth. The present life of a person is considered to be the result of his or her past life, where past life includes not only the past of current life, but also lives that were lived before the present birth. The present life becomes past life after death, and with other past lives, determines the course of the next life. It is really the action or *karma* that is responsible for the "life after life" cycle. The *karmas* of the individual determine what life lies ahead, whether here or hereafter. But *bhaktas* or devotees believe that the karmic course can be changed by God's grace.

The Story expresses the belief that there are people in *dukha* or "suffering" because of their own bad *karmas* or sins *(papa);* but that something can be done by God so that those people may improve their *karmas.* Improvement of *karmas* comes through *punya* or good deeds leading to enjoyment of material pleasures and receiving of *moksha* at the end. The Story recommends the Worship to achieve *sukha* or happiness in this life and *moksha* hereafter.

The concept of *moksha* in this Worship is not identical with that in other views. For example, in the Vedanta of the Upanishads, when the individual *(atman)* realizes his or her identity with the one Universal Self *(Brahman)* he or she is considered *mukta* or liberated. This Vedantic experience can be achieved while living. Patanjali's yoga requires the individual to practice constant meditation or *samadhi* for achieving his or her independence or *kaivalya,* which, again, is live liberation.

A most interesting *moksha* view to compare with that of the Story would be from the *Gita.* Krishna is the link here, since the *Gita* shares him with the Story. The *Gita* offers several options that vary according to the needs of the individual in question. But the real alternative offered by the *Gita* is in the philosophy of *karma yoga* or action psychology. It is about enjoying work without stress. Philosophically this yoga leads to *moksha.* We will briefly discuss both aspects below.

The *Gita* presents the case of Arjuna, a royal class or *Kshatriya* warrior who becomes depressed when he has to do his job of fighting in a war. He is not afraid of fighting but of its consequences. What bothers him about this war is the uncertainty of loss or gain, victory or defeat, pride or humiliation, pain or pleasure, and other such dualities *(dvandvas).* He develops a sense of guilt and is willing to be dead rather than fight.

Then comes Krishna as a psychologist and philosopher counseling Arjuna to remain neutral or same *(sama)* through all kinds of dualities. It is "expectations" that have to be eliminated while at work. Absence of expectation will reduce job anxiety and improve one's efficiency, eventually yielding better results.

This work psychology is called *nishkama-karma-yoga* "desireless-action-yoga." One must work for the sake of work (*karma*) and not for work's "fruit" (*phala*). A person who works with this yoga is liberated here and hereafter. The *Gita* teaches that it is the attachment to the reward of actions, not the actions or *karmas* themselves, that binds a person in this life as well as afterward. The great appeal of the *Gita* to the intellectual is that it involves the individual and his or her "attitude" (*bhava*) for liberation only; it does not require any formal, ritualistic, social, and material behavior, but is purely one's own private affair.

The Story and the Worship, on the other hand, support *bhakti* only, a ritualistic *bhakti* that requires public participation. It is the sociability of this *bhakti* that gives it strength. The way in which it is rewarding for the worshipper and for his or her society requires deeper analysis that will take place in the last part of this book. Suffice it to note here that it is not like the informal, internal, and individualistic *bhakti* of the *Gita*.

To recapitulate, the basic difference between the *Gita* and the Story is that the *Gita* insists on the *nishkama* or "desireless" *bhakti,* the Story on the *sakama* or "with desire" *bhakti.* For the *Gita,* the bhakti "with desire" is inferior and cannot help the devotee attain *shanti* and *mukti;* that is, peace and liberation. The Story includes devotee characters who are shown to have earned riches and contentment, rewards that an average person must look for. In the end, these characters receive *moksha* as the last reward after rebirth. Through these characters, we are told that realistically *artha* "wealth" and *kama* "fulfillment of desires" are as important as *dharma* and *moksha.* That is, the Story and the Worship stand for balancing these four goals in life.

The *Gita* supports *jnana* or knowledge also as another alternative for liberation called *Brahma-nirvana.* This means simply experience of *Atman* (or the individual self) as Brahman (or the universal Self). Such a liberation is non-dualistic and is the ultimate experience. But this is not the kind of "nirvana in Brahman" suggested by the characters in the Story. First it must be taken into account that *bhakti* means "sharing," which requires duality. Here God and devotee share with each other. Even when the devotee receives *mukti,* it is of the "shared" type. There are basically four shared *muktis* in *bhakti:* sharing "proximity" (*sannidhya*) of God; sharing the "world" (*salokya*) of God; sharing the "form" (*sarupya*) of God; and sharing the "union" (*sayujya*) with God.

In *moksha* the devotee is in contact with, not identical with God. The Worship supports this view, although there are other views that differ regarding the state of *moksha*. During the *puja*, however, certain practices may be considered symbolic of uniting the worshipper with God. The highest unity, in a Vedantic sense, would be total absorption of the worshipper's identity with that of the ultimate divinity. This could be associated with the "life establishment" ceremony. It is not necessary, however, to perform this ceremony with those features that suggest total oneness of the worshipper with God.

But the four shared *muktis* are clearly ritualized during the *puja*. For example, what may appear to be total identity or oneness of the worshipper and God may be interpreted as *sayujya*, or union with God. If the life of the worshipper is considered in this process to be identical with that of God, then it could be *sarupya mukti,* meaning one has assumed the form of the other.

It is obligatory in the *puja* to invite God to sit on the altar in the form of the icon or its non-iconic equivalent. Now the worshipper is in the proximity of God, known as *sannidhya* or *samipya* "closeness." Also, the *puja* place is shared by the worshipper and God, which symbolizes the *salokya* or identical place-sharing. Thus, these four *muktis* are achieved while the worshipper is alive even though they represent only their metaphoric sense in the performance.

The metaphoric sense, nevertheless, is capable of liberating the worshipper from the stress that he or she has been experiencing in the actualization of a particular desire or dream. The worshipper feels relieved in believing that God came here to the *puja* place to take care of that desire. Virtually every step taken in the *puja* is expected to produce the effect of relief, not only for the worshipper but for the other family members. Thus, the presence of others during the *puja* performance gives the worshipper their moral support in quest of his or her dream.

Three other parts of the performance are intended to produce further relief. These are the episodes pertaining to those characters who performed this *puja* the first time. Following these, there is devotional music and eating of the sacred food.

The episodes are called stories or *katha,* and are arranged in a dramatic style. First the "problem" is presented, which is *dukha* or pain. The solution to be sought is *sukha* or pleasure. The characters in the beginning go through the cycles of *dukha* or *sukha,* creating in general less tension. In the middle of this, comes the episode of the merchant who goes through more cycles of *dukha* and *sukha* than any other character in the Story. The tension curve rises to its peak in this episode. The end of the last episode brings the tension curve to its lowest point. These episodes or stories must be read publicly; in fact, this reading is obligatory in the performance. Listeners are expected to react emotionally with a great degree of empathy for the characters. The more empathy the listener experiences the more sense of "release" or *mukti* he or she is likely to experience.

The expression of such release is visible on the faces of the worshipper and others when they sing devotional songs. A devotional song is called *bhajana* or *bhajan,* which relates to the word *bhakti.* That the attendants experience devotion is observed in such non-verbal behavior as tears in their eyes or an overall tranquility *(shanti)* on their faces. When such expressions are observed among all the participants they are assumed to be enjoying the emotion known as *bhakti rasa.*

The term *rasa* means "juice, chemical fluid, flavor, taste, emotion, joy." It is an artistic concept first presented in an ancient book known as *Natya Shastra* or "Dramatic Science." The book supposedly was authored by a man named Bharata and deals with drama, theatre, musicology, and literary theory. In this book, the author presents the theory of *rasa* in the particular context of dramatic performance, but it covers the enjoyment of any art form. The theory maintains that when an artwork is presented to others, they are likely to experience one or more *rasas* or emotions. There are eight major *rasas* or emotions: love, pride, humor, wonder, hate, anger, fear, and sorrow. The human body releases some fluids when emotion is intense; e.g., tears are shed when sorrow is felt, or sweat is secreted when fear attacks. Bharata calls such an aesthetic or artistic experience *rasa-nishpatti* "rasa release," which can also be translated as "fluid secretion."

Rasa release or aesthetic experience is equated with live liberation, even though it lasts only as long as an artistic performance, for example, a play on the stage. The *rasa*-experience is pure joy or *ananda.* It does not arise from actual events in the life of the experiencer, but is aroused by an art performance experienced by watching, reading, listening, etc. Since the performance is not directly associated with the experiencer's life events, he or she can enjoy it with a detached sense. Even sorrow can become joy, when presented through a work of art. Since this joy comes out of such detachment it is equated with the bliss (*ananda*) that is experienced in live liberation or *jivan mukti*. In a more realistic sense *rasa* release can be understood as stress relief from chemical changes in the body through artistic expression.

The advocates of *bhakti* philosophy maintain that there is another unique *rasa;* that is, *bhakti rasa* or the "devotion emotion." Many visible changes commonly take place in the bodies of devotees when the devotional songs, stories, and worships are presented. These are devotional art forms that arouse the emotion of *bhakti* in the *bhaktas,* providing immediate release and momentary forgetting of worldly problems and the emotions attached to them. In fact, *bhakti* is an emotional approach to realizing God's presence within. God has been called *rasa;* the famous saying in Sanskrit is "Emotion indeed (is) He" (*raso vai sah*) The liberation in *bhakti* is achieved through emotion rather than *jnana*-rationalization, reason, logic, or knowledge. The existence of this emotion is observed, for example, when a devotee's eyes release tears, which are liberating or healing fluids as the word *rasa* suggests (compare *rasa* as in *rasayana* "chemical, medicine").

THE LIBERATED CHARACTERS

The view in the Story is that those who experience the *bhakti rasa* or "devotion emotion" will eventually receive *moksha*. The Story has characters who are *mukta* "liberated" as they received *mukti* "liberation." This *mukti* or *moksha* is the experience of permanent contact, not identity, with God. The Story, for example, says that "he enjoyed happiness in this world and finally went to Satya's city." To be with God in his place is called *salokya mukti*. The worshippers may get *moksha* not necessarily at the end of their present lives, but after the next lives. The following Puranic characters are examples of *mukta* or "liberated" *bhaktas*.

(1) **Sudaman:** As a poor Brahmin boy, Sudaman studied with Krishna at a hermitage. One morning their guru's wife sent them out to gather wood from a nearby forest. The two boys were caught up in a rainstorm. Sudaman, holding Krishna's hand, tried to get out of the forest. But they

were forced to spend the whole night there. Next day their guru found them together and brought them home safely.

After the great war of the *Mahabharata,* it is believed that Krishna established his capital in Dvaraka, the modern Dwaraka, a city on the western coast of India. But Sudaman and his family continued to live in the north in great poverty. His wife asked him to go to see his classmate and friend Krishna for financial aid. So Sudaman went to Dvaraka where the two friends met with great joy.

Krishna introduced Sudaman to his wife Rukmini. Sudaman gave Krishna a small package of puffed rice, the only gift he could afford to bring. Krishna took a handful of the rice and ate it, then took another handful, but Rukmini stopped him from eating the second serving. Sudaman lived for some time in Dvaraka as an honored guest of Krishna, and he left for home with all the verbal courtesy of Krishna and Rukmini, but no material or financial help.

Deeply depressed, he reached home after a long journey, only to find to his dismay that the poor cottage he owned was not there; in its place now was a palace. But his wife and children greeted him at the gate of the palace and led him inside to tell him that it was his own palace. That big a favor Krishna did for only one handful of rice.

(2) **Dasharatha** and **Guha**: These two characters are from Valmiki's *Ramayana.*

Dasharatha, the king of Ayodhya, had four sons. Rama was born from his first wife Kausalya, Lakshmana and Shatrughna were born from his second wife Sumitra, and Bharata was born from his third wife Kaikeyi. Rama was the oldest and heir-apparent. But Kaikeyi requested Dasharatha to grant her two wishes that he had promised to her long ago: one to make her son Bharata his heir-apparent and the other was to exile Rama for fourteen years.

Dasharatha tried to dissuade her but failed and then granted her two wishes with heavy heart. Rama gladly accepted the exile, even though Dasharatha urged him to disobey. Lakshmana and Rama's wife, Sita accompanied Rama in his exile. When all this happened, Bharata and Shatrughna were not home, and Dasharatha, saddened by Rama's departure, died within a few days.

When Rama, Sita, and Lakshmana arrived at the bank of the Ganges, they were greeted and honored by Guha, chief of the Nishada tribe. Rama wanted to go across the river, and Guha himself took the three across in his boat. Later when Bharata and Shatrughna went out in search of Rama, Guha helped in locating him. Here Rama, an Aryan, and Guha, a Nishada or Austric, represent inter-ethnic cooperation.

In the Story, Dasharatha is considered a great devotee of Vishnu. This is why Rama, an avatar of Vishnu, chose him to be his mortal father. In particular, Dasharatha worshipped Vishnu in the temple of Ranganatha, which is in southern India near Madras. This is an important point for the history of *bhakti*. It is well-established fact that the *bhakti* movement came to northern India from the south. Not only great philosophers such as Shankara and Ramanuja, but also great Shaiva and Vaishnava saints, the *Nayanars* and *Alvars* respectively, came from the south. The story recognizes the significance of this southern influence on the north when it includes Dasharatha's visit to a temple. The southern temples during the period of the *Skanda Purana* were the inspirational sources for the practice of *bhakti* in the form of *puja* or worship. The Puranic *bhakti* is considered to be Dravidian (*Dravidi*) in origin, meaning that it originated in the south. Later, great *bhakti* philosophers such as Madhva and Vallabha were also southern Indians. Here pilgrimage and temple worship encourage contact between the people of the various regions.

(3) **Moradhvaja**: He was king of Ratnapura. Once he performed a *yajna* called *ashvamedha* "horse-sacrifice." By this ritual a king would let a ceremonial horse cross into another kingdom in order to establish his dominance over that kingdom. The other king, however, could challenge the horse-owner, resulting in a battle to settle the issues of supremacy and sovereignty.

Yudhishthira, oldest brother of Arjuna and king of Hastinapura, performed such a horse ritual at the same time as Moradhvaja. Consequently a battle took place between Moradhvaja's son Tamradhvaja and Arjuna who was accompanied by Krishna. Tamradhvaja left Arjuna and Krishna unconscious in the battlefield and took their ceremonial horse away with him.

When the two wounded friends became conscious they decided to see Moradhvaja. They disguised themselves as two Brahmins, Krishna as a guru, and Arjuna as his disciple. Moradhvaja welcomed them in his palace with great courtesy and asked the reason for their visit. Krishna told

Moradhvaja that a lion wanted to devour the other Brahmin's son. The lion, however, would accept the right half of Moradhvaja's body in exchange for the Brahmin boy, but the king's body must be cut into two halves with a saw by his wife and son. The king gladly agreed. His son and wife wanted to take his place, but Krishna did not accept that.

When Moradhvaja's body was being sawed by his wife and son, a teardrop fell from his left eye. Upon seeing that, Krishna told him that his body was not acceptable because a gift was no good if given with sadness. Moradhvaja replied that the left half of his body was sad because it was not so fortunate as the right half, which would be useful for his benevolent act.

Moved by Moradhvaja's reply, Krishna and Arjuna revealed their real identity. With one touch of Krishna, the body of the king became normal and healthy. He asked Krishna and Arjuna to forgive his son's ignorance of them and returned the ceremonial horse with great honor. Thus Krishna proved to Arjuna that Moradhvaja was as good a devotee as Arjuna himself.

(4) **Svayambhuva Manu**: This is the first Manu, who created humans. He is called *Svayambhuva* "son of the self-born." Here Brahma is the self-born, and his son is Manu. As said earlier, there are fourteen Manu-intervals or Manu-periods of time that make a day of Brahma. Six such periods have already passed. We are in the seventh period. After seven more Manu periods Brahma's day is over. The Brahma's night lasts as long as his day. The day starts again with the first Manu period, ruled by another Manu.

Thus the Story suggests that this *puja* is good for all ages. Liberation takes place in any age. This Manu belongs to the *Satya Yuga,* Dasharatha and Guha to the *Treta,* Sudaman and Moradhvaja to the *Dvapara.* Now it is recommended for the Age of *Kali.*

PART III

THE STORY TEXT

A popular print of Satya Narayana used in the puja. Note, at the bottom of the picture, the U.S. dollars placed as offerings.

Note on Translation

This text translation of the *Skanda Purana* consists of five *adhyayas* or chapters. Some handbooks present the text in seven. Performance procedures are suggested in the first chapter but handbooks are usually patterned after the common frame of the most auspicious ceremonies. Reading of the following chapters takes place in the middle of the procedures, which are discussed in Part IV.

FIRST CHAPTER

1. Vyasa said: Once in the Naimisha forest Shaunaka and all other rishis indeed questioned Suta, the knower of the Puranas.

2. The rishis said: By which vrata and tapa is procured the desired fruit? We wish to hear all about that. O great sage! Tell us!

3. Suta said: Narada too asked the Lord, the spouse of Lakshmi. Listen attentively what He said to the godly sage.

4. Once Yogi Narada with the intention of helping others wandering in various other worlds reached the earthly world.

5. Then he saw people with various miseries born in various species troubled due to their own karmas.

6. "By what means would be the sure destruction of their misery?" Thus concerned in his mind he went then to the world of Vishnu.

7. There was Lord Narayana with shining complexion and four arms adorned with conch, discus, mace, lotus, and garland of wild flowers.

8. Seeing the Lord of all the gods he began to offer praise. Narada said, "Salutation to you who has the form beyond speech and mind, who has infinite power,

9. Who had no beginning, middle and end, who is without qualities, yet who owns qualities, who is the cause of all the beings, who is destroyer of the agony of all the devotees."

10. Vishnu heard the praise, then spoke to Narada. The Lord said, "For what purpose of yours have you come here? What is in your mind?

11. O blessed one! Tell me! Then I will tell you all." Narada said, "On the earth all beings are with many miseries. Born in various species they are being cooked by their sinful deeds.

12. So Lord! Tell me how with a little effort that can be extinguished. I wish to hear about it all if you have mercy upon me."

13. The Lord said, "You have asked very well with the intention of helping others. Listen now about that by doing which the person is released from attachment. I tell you now,

14. There is a vrata which is highly rewarding in heaven and earth, but inaccessible. Due to your affection, O son, I bring it to light now,

15. This is the Satya Narayana vrata; having performed it well, one immediately enjoys happiness and attains liberation hereafter."

16. After hearing the words of the Lord sage Narada spoke. Narada said, "What is the fruit? What is the method? And who did that vrata?

17. Then tell me all in detail when the vrata should be done." The Lord said, "This calms pain, sorrow, etc., increases wealth and prosperity,

18. It produces good fortune and offspring, and gives victory everywhere. On any day when a person is full of devotion and faith, he

19. Should worship Lord Satya Narayana that evening with Brahmins and relatives dutifully,

20. He should offer naivedya with one and a quarter unit of food, bananas, ghee, milk, and wheat flour,

21. Or in their absence mix rice flour and sugar, including molasses, with one quarter unit of all the eatables and offer them,

22. And give dakshina to the priest after hearing the story with the people. And then feed the Brahmins including the relatives,

23. He should eat prasada with devotion and engage in dancing, singing, etc. Then all should go to their homes while remembering Lord Satya Narayana.

24. Doing thus, fulfillment of the wish of the people would definitely take place. Particularly in the Age of Kali this is the short solution on the earth."

Thus ends the first chapter of the Satya Narayana Worship Story in the Reva Section of the Skanda Purana.

SECOND CHAPTER

1. Suta said: Now I will tell you about the person who did it first, O Brahmin! A very poor Brahmin lived in the beautiful Kashi city.

2. Suffering from hunger and thirst he always wandered on the earth. On seeing the sad Brahmin the Lord, who is fond of the Brahmins,

3. Assumed the form of an old Brahmin and asked the Brahmin respectfully, "For what purpose do you wander on the earth, always sad?

4. I want to hear all about that. Please tell me, O great Brahmin!" The Brahmin said, "I am a very poor Brahmin. I wander on the earth for alms.

5. If you know any solution then kindly tell me, sir!" The old Brahmin said, "Satya Narayana Vishnu is the giver of the desired fruit.

6. O Brahmin! you perform His worship, the best vrata, by doing which a human becomes free from all sorrows."

7. And after explaining very carefully to the Brahmin the vrata's method also, Satya Narayana, as the old man, vanished right there.

8. "I will perform the vrata as told by that Brahmin," thus decided this Brahmin and he was unable to sleep during the night.

9. Thereafter he got up in the morning. "I will do the Satya Narayana vrata"; thus the Brahmin vowed and went out for alms.

10. On that very day the Brahmin received ample materials. With them he, accompanied by his relatives, performed the vrata of Satya.

11. That noble Brahmin became free from all sorrows and was endowed with all riches due to the power of this vrata.

12. Since that time he did the vrata every month. Doing thus the vrata of Narayana

13. The great Brahmin, free from all sins, obtained the inaccessible moksha. When the Brahmins will perform this vrata on the earth

14. Right then the person's entire sorrow will be destroyed. Thus what was said by Narayana to Narada, the great soul,

15. That I have told you, O Brahmins, what else do I say now? The rishis inquired, "Who else performed it after hearing from that Brahmin?

16. We want to hear about it all. Our faith is born." Suta said: Listen, O sages, about who else did the vrata on the earth! Once that noble Brahmin according to his wealthy capacity

17. Was engaged in doing the vrata with his relatives. Just at this time one woodseller came around there.

18. And he placed his wood outside and came inside the house of the Brahmin. And when distressed by thirst he saw the vrata being performed by the Brahmin.

19. He bowed and asked the Brahmin "What is it being done by you? What fruit do you get after doing this? Tell me in detail, sir."

20. The Brahmin said, "This is Satya Narayana's vrata that grants whatever desired. Due to its blessing I have all the big wealth and riches."

21. Having known from him about this vrata the woodseller became very happy. After drinking water and eating prasada he went to the city.

22. Thinking of Lord Satya Narayana mentally, "Whatever money I will get today by selling the wood in the village,

23. With that I will perform the best vrata of Lord Satya Narayana." Thinking recurrently like this in his mind, he placed the wood on his head.

24. And went to the beautiful city where rich people lived. That day he received a doubly high price for his wood.

25. So he was happy in his heart. With very ripe bananas, sugar, ghee, milk and wheat flour,

26. Together he took one unit and a quarter more of them and went to his home. Then he invited his relatives and performed the vrata according to the method.

27. By the power of that vrata he was blessed with wealth and children. After enjoying happiness in this world he went to the city of Satya in the end.

Thus ends the second chapter of the Satya Narayana Worship Story in the Reva Section of the Skanda Purana.

THIRD CHAPTER

1. Suta said: I will speak further. Listen, O best sages! In old times there was a great intelligent king named Ulkamukha.

2. He was master of his senses and a truth-speaker. He went to temples. Every day he gave money to learned Brahmins and made them happy.

3. His wife was charming, lotus-faced, and devoted. They performed the vrata on the bank of the river Bhadrashila.

4. In the meantime a merchant came there for the purpose of business. He was loaded with many riches.

5. He anchored his boat on that bank and went toward the king. When he saw the king performing the vrata he asked him humbly.

6. The merchant spoke, "What is this you are doing, O King, with a dedicated mind? Bring it to light, as I would like to hear about it all at this time."

7. The king said, "O merchant! This is an extremely powerful Vishnu's worship and vrata being performed in the company of our relatives with the wish of having children, etc."

8. The merchant heard the words of the king and replied with respect, "Tell me all, O King! I will do as explained by you,

9. I too have no child. With this I will indeed have one." Thereafter he returned from business and came home with great joy.

10. He told his wife about the whole vrata that grants offspring. "Then I will do the vrata when I am about to have a child."

11. Thus that noble merchant said to his wife Lilavati. One day the devout wife Lilavati,

12. Delighted in the company of her husband, she dedicated herself to the family duty. His wife, with the blessing of the Lord, became pregnant.

13. In the tenth month was born her daughter, a gem. Day by day she grew up like the moon in the bright half of the month.

14. By name she was Kalavati, as was done in her naming ceremony. Then Lilavati asked her husband with sweet words,

15. "Why don't you do the vrata that you long ago promised to do?" The merchant said, "I will do it at the time of her marriage, dear!"

16. Thus he assured his wife and went toward the city. Later on Kalavati grew up big in her father's home.

17. When the merchant saw his daughter in the city with her girlfriends, he thought it over quickly and sent out a knowledgeable messenger.

18. "Consider a noble bridegroom for the girl to wed." Thus instructed by him the messenger went to the city of Kanchana.

19. From there he picked up a merchant boy and came back. After seeing the handsome, virtuous merchant boy,

20. Completely satisfied in his mind and accompanied by relatives and friends, he gave away his daughter to the merchant boy as prescribed by the laws.

21. Then unfortunately he forgot the great vrata. The Lord became displeased with him at her wedding time.

22. Thereafter as determined by time the merchant, who was very efficient in his work, left for his business immediately with his son-in-law.

23. He went to the pretty city, Ratnasarapura, near the sea and quickly did business aided by his noble son-in-law.

24. After the two went to King Chandraketu's pretty city, Lord Satya Narayana in the meantime,

25. Seeing him deviated from his vow, put a curse on him, "A very harsh and unbearable sadness will occur to him."

26. One day a thief took away a property of the king and came right where the two merchants were stationed.

27. Then, terrified in his mind by seeing the officers running after him, the thief placed the property right there and quickly disappeared.

28. Afterwards the officers arrived where the gentle merchant was. On seeing the king's property there they arrested the two merchants and took them away.

29. Hurrying back with happiness they announced near the king, saying, "We have brought the two thieves, Your Majesty! After checking them, instruct us."

30. Ordered by the king thereafter, they quickly tied the two and placed them in a tight security prison without any consideration.

31. Due to the maya of Lord Satya their voices were not heard. Then their property was taken away by King Chandraketu.

32. And in their home, due to the curse the merchant's wife became extremely miserable. Whatever was in the house was stolen by a thief.

33. She was stricken by diseases and disorders and agonized by hunger and thirst. Desperately looking for food, she roamed from house to house.

34. Kalavati, the daughter, too, roamed around every day. One day, pained by hunger, she went to a Brahmin's house.

35. Upon entering there, she saw the vrata of Satya Narayana. She sat there, heard the story while praying. After the prasada she returned home during the night.

36. The mother said to her daughter, Kalavati, affectionately, "Dear, where were you so late at night? What is in your mind?"

37. Kalavati, the daughter, replied to her mother quickly, "In a Brahmin's home I saw a vrata that grants attainment of the desired wish."

38. After hearing the statement of her daughter, she prepared herself to perform the vrata. And indeed that wife of the merchant,

39. That very devout woman, with her relatives and friends, performed the vrata of Satya Narayana. "Let my husband and son-in-law come home soon,

40. And you must forgive the mistake of my husband and son-in-law." By this vrata Satya Narayana was pleased again.

41. He appeared in the dream of the great King Chandraketu, "Release in the morning the two merchant prisoners, O noble King!

42. You ought to give them now all the wealth you took from them. Otherwise I will destroy you with your kingdom, wealth and children."

43. Saying thus to the king, the Lord disappeared. And later in the morning the king with his people,

44. Sat in conference and told them his dream. "I release immediately the two imprisoned great merchants."

45. Thus they heard the words of the king and released the two merchants. When they brought them in front of the king, they said humbly,

46. "We have brought the two merchants just free from chains." Then the two businessmen bowed to the noble King Chandraketu.

47. Both of them, remembering the past events, did not utter a word, as they were horror-stricken. Looking at the merchants, the king said respectfully,

48. "Due to destiny you suffered great pain. Now there is no fear." Then he ordered their release providing them with haircuts, etc.

49. And the king gave them clothes and jewels, rewarded them a great deal and, after honoring the two merchants, he gratified them much with words.

50. He doubled the property that was taken from them before and gave it back. And finally the king said, "Both of you go home!"

51. Then one bowed to the king and said, "We must go, with your favor." Saying this, both great businessmen left for their home.

Thus ends the third chapter of the Satya Narayana Worship Story in the Reva Section of the Skanda Purana.

FOURTH CHAPTER

1. Suta said: The merchant started the journey with auspicious prayers. He gave money to Brahmins and then indeed went to the city.

2. After the merchant went a little way, Lord Satya Narayana expressed curiosity, saying, "O merchant! What is your boat loaded with?"

3. Then the two proud businessmen laughed with disrespect, "Why do you ask so, O monk? Do you want to take off with our money?

4. Just plants, leaves, etc. are there in my boat." Hearing these unkind words, "Let your words be true,"

5. Thus said the monk and went away quickly from the vicinity. Afterwards He went a little further and stayed near the sea.

6. Then when the monk went away, the merchant finished his daily routine and saw the boat raised up, which surprised him greatly.

7. He fell on the ground unconscious when he saw plants, leaves, etc. there. After regaining consciousness the merchant was overcome with worry.

8. At that time his daughter's husband spoke these words, "Why are you going through this grief? This is the curse put on you by that monk.

9. Everything can be done by Him. There is no doubt about this. Let us, therefore, take refuge in Him. Our desired wish will take place."

10. On hearing the words of his son-in-law he proceeded in His direction. And after seeing the monk he bowed with devotion and spoke with reference.

11. "Forgive my crime that I lied in your presence." Saying this he bowed again and again, and was greatly overwhelmed by grief.

12. Then the monk spoke these words after seeing him wailing, "Don't cry. Listen to my words. You have turned away from my worship,

13. O evil-minded one! You have received pain again and again by my order." When he heard these words of the Lord, he started offering this praise.

14. "Due to your maya even Brahma, the Creator, and all other gods living in the three worlds are deluded. They do not know your qualities and form. This is a wonder, Lord!

15. I am a fool. How could I know you? I am deluded by your maya. Be pleased, I will worship you according to my power and prosperity,

16. Let all the wealth be there as it was before! Save me! I have taken refuge in you." The Lord of the devotees heard the words full of devotion and they pleased Him.

17. The Lord bestowed upon him the desired blessing and vanished right there. Then the merchant climbed the boat and saw it filled with wealth.

18. "With the Lord's grace my wish was granted." Thus he said, and then with his people he performed worship as prescribed.

19. And he became fully happy from the Lord's favor. He boarded the boat carefully and left for his homeland.

20. Then the merchant said to his son-in-law, "Look at my city Ratnapuri." And he sent out a messenger who was guard of his wealth.

21. This messenger went to the city and saw the merchant's wife. He spoke the desired words after bowing with folded hands.

22. "Near this very city the merchant with his son-in-law has come with a party of friends and many riches."

23. Hearing this sentence from the mouth of the messenger, the devout wife was overjoyed. Then she performed the Satya worship and spoke to her daughter,

24. "I am going to see the merchant, and you come soon too." Thus hearing the words of her mother, she performed and completed the vrata.

25. But, abandoning the prasada, she too proceeded to see her husband. Due to that, Lord Satya was displeased, and her husband and the boat,

26. Were taken away, along with the riches, and then drowned in that water by Him. Afterwards, when Kalavati did not see her husband,

27. She fell on the ground there, crying with great sorrow. Upon seeing the situation with the boat and the extremely sad daughter,

28. With horrified mind the merchant spoke, "What is this great surprise?" And all the sailors became concerned.

29. Then, watching the daughter, Lilavati became bewildered. She cried with great grief and said this to her husband,

30. "At this time, how did he, with the boat, become invisible? I don't know due to which deity's disrespect that was taken away!

31. Or who is able to know the importance of Lord Satya?" Thus saying she wailed with her relatives.

32. Then Lilavati placed her daughter in her lap and wept. After a while Kalavati, the daughter, grieving from the loss of her husband,

33. Took his sandals and decided in her mind to follow him. Seeing the conduct of his daughter, the gentle merchant, accompanied by his wife,

34. Saddened by extreme grief, pondered over dharma as he knew it. "Either it has been taken away by Lord Satya or I am deluded by His maya.

35. I will perform the puja of Satya according to my wealth and property." Thus he told his intention to all whom he had gathered around.

36. And he prostrated to Lord Satya like a stick on the ground. Then Lord Satya, the protector of the meek, was pleased.

37. And He, who is affectionate to the devotees, said these words compassionately, "Your daughter abandoned the prasada and proceeded to see her husband.

38. Therefore, that girl's husband has indeed become invisible. If she goes home, eats the prasada and comes back, then,

39. She will regain her husband, O merchant. There is no doubt." The girl heard these words originating from the sky.

40. She quickly went home and ate the prasada. Later she came back again and saw her husband.

Thus ends the fourth chapter of the Satya Narayana Worship
Story in the Reva Section of the Skanda Purana.

FIFTH CHAPTER

1. Suta said: Now I will say ahead. Listen, O great sages! There was
    one king Tungadhvaja who was dedicated to the protection of his
    subjects.

2. He ignored the prasada of Lord Satya and received unhappiness. Once
    he went to a forest, killed many kinds of animals,

3. And came to a banyan tree under which he saw Satya's service being
    performed by the cowherds, who were contented and devoted in the
    company of their friends.

4. Even though he saw so, he did not go near, nor did he bow. Then all
    the cowherds placed the sacred food in front of the king,

5. And came back. Then they all ate as wished. Thereafter the king
    abandoned the sacred food and received unhappiness.

6. His hundred sons were destroyed as well as whatever wealth and
    property he had. "All that has been destroyed by Lord Satya. Such is
    my determination,

7. "So I am going where the worship of the Lord was held." Thus he
    determined in his mind and went to the cowherds.

8. Then, in the company of the cowherds, the king, with devotion and
    faith, performed the puja of Lord Satya as prescribed.

9. By Lord Satya's grace he became endowed with health and sons. In
    this world he enjoyed happiness and in the end he went to the city of
    Satya.

10. One who performs this extremely invaluable Satya vrata and hears with devotion the sacred and rewarding story,

11. Wealth and prosperity will be his by Satya's grace. The poor gains money, the bonded is released from bonds,

12. Very truly, the fearful is relieved from fear. There is no doubt. Such a person would enjoy the desired fruit and go in the end to the city of Satya.

13. Thus has been said to you, O Brahmins, by performing the Satya Narayana vrata a human becomes free from all sorrows.

14. Especially in this dark age the worship of Truth is fruitful. Some call It "Time," "Truth," "Supreme,"

15. And some "Satya Narayana," and even others "True God." He assumes various forms and grants the wishes of all.

16. In the Age of Kali the ancient Satya vrata itself will be the form assumed by Lord Vishnu that will grant the wishes of all.

17. One who reads or hears it every day, O great sages, his sins are destroyed by the True God's grace.

18. Now, O lords of the sages, I will tell you the other incarnations of those who first did the vrata of Satya Narayana.

19. Shatananda, the great intellectual, became the Brahmin Sudaman. In that incarnation he meditated on Lord Krishna and obtained moksha.

20. The woodseller became Bhilla Guharaja. In that incarnation he served Lord Rama and indeed went to moksha.

21. Ulkamukha, the great king, became King Dasharatha. He worshipped Lord Ranganatha and then went to the sacred Vaikuntha.

22. The dutiful and truthful merchant became Moradhvaja. He offered one half of his body, having cut it by a saw, and thus obtained moksha.

23. Tungadhvaja, the great king, was known as Svayambhuva, who performed all the duties assigned by God and then went to the holy Vaikuntha.

Thus ends the fifth chapter of the Satya Narayana Worship Story in the Reva Section of the Skanda Purana.

PART IV

THE WORSHIP PROCEDURES

Some sacred materials used in the puja: a coconut over a water-pot on a plate with rice grains, another plate with rice grains and a wick, a lamp lit beside the black Shalagrama set on top of a brass holder for the purpose of offerings.

SOME PROGRAMMATIC REMARKS

The Story does not give the details of how the Worship or *puja* of Satya Narayana should be performed. But in the Story's opening episode the following general guidelines are given:

> On any day when a person is full of devotion and faith he should dutifully worship Lord Satya Narayana that evening with Brahmins and relatives. He should offer naivedya consisting of one and an extra quarter unit of food, bananas, clarified butter, milk, and wheat flour. Or, in their absence, mix rice flour and sugar including an extra quarter of all the eatables; offer them to the Lord. Then give a cash gift to the priest after hearing the story with the audience. Then feed the Brahmins and relatives. The worshipper should eat the sacramental food with faith. Then dancing, singing, etc., should take place. In the end all should go home remembering the Lord.

In the Worship, not in the Story, we find a vow for the worshipper. Usually, the vows are more or less identical in all the pujas, but the present Worship's vow is not as elaborate as elsewhere. The vow serves as the plan or program for the puja as well as the commitment to it. The word for vow is *sankalpa* or *samkalpa,* which means "vow, determination, firm plan, decision, commitment." Most handbooks contain a simple vow to be read by the worshipper in the beginning. It is as follows:

> I, such and such person of such and such lineage, for the fulfillment of my whole wish preceded by the extinction of all the difficulties and alleviation of all the distresses accompanied by all the necessary materials, preceded by the worship of Ganesha, Gauri, Varuna, the five deities, the world guardians starting with Ganapati, and the Sun with the nine planetary gods—first these parts done—will do the holy Satya Narayana Worship and the Story reading.

Thus the general guidelines from the Story section list the sacred materials and the deities to be worshipped in the entire performance. Before the vow it is customary to do an auspicious recitation called *svastivachana.*

Usually the order given in the vow is followed, with a few changes here and there, depending on the discretion of the worshipper or the priest. The following *pujas* are the most common in an elaborate performance: (1) The Ganesha; (2) the Varuna or Kalasha; (3) the planetary; (4) the big five deities; (5) the Lokapala; (6) the Satya Narayana *puja* and reading; (7) the *havana*.

The vow implies that the *pujas* before the Satya Narayana *puja* are the parts to be completed first. The major one is the Satya Narayana *puja*, which is performed after the minor *pujas*. Such a scheme, according to which the main deity is honored after the supporting deities, was called earlier multimonotheistic worship. It should be noted here that a few other minor *pujas* or ceremonies can be inserted in varying order before the major *puja*. For example, the "life-establishment" *(prana-pratishtha)* ceremony can be performed just before the Ganesha or the Satya Narayana *puja*. The *Matrika* or *Vasordhara pujas* can be added at any time after the Kalasha *puja*. A small Ganapati or Ganesha *puja*, as the vow suggests, may be performed again after all minor *pujas* have been completed. Such a small Ganapati *puja* later marks the beginning of the Satya Narayana *puja*.

A great deal of flexibility is allowed in this *puja*, depending on circumstances. For example, if the priest is an accomplished professional, referred to as *pandit* (pundit), he is likely to go beyond the suggestions of the handbook and do the *puja* in a grand style. But if the worshipper is doing the *puja* himself or herself then the performance is simpler, shorter, and more economical. If the worshipper knows Sanskrit and the related religious literature, however, the *puja* may be quite elaborate. There are handbooks in the various regional languages with no Sanskritic contents in them, which means that a priestly knowledge is not essential in order to perform the Satya Narayana *puja*. In the absence of the Sanskritic contents, the minor *pujas* are optional; a simple *puja* of Vishnu (or other forms such as Krishna) is considered adequate.

The *puja* contents to be discussed below are part of the grand or elaborate style. It is not possible here to give all the Sanskritic contents. But I have included in my own translation the most important mantras with necessary explanations or comments. A cross-reference or occasional repetition of almost the same information is intended for clarification.

THE SACRED PLACE AND ITEMS

The guidelines imply that this *puja*, i.e. the service to honor the deity, can be performed anywhere. Most often one's own home is the best place. Established shrines and temples are common. An outdoor *puja* is also possible, preferably under a big tree or canopy. It is important that the designated place be washed thoroughly with water before the *puja*. Materials made with leather, shoes, for example, are not allowed within the *puja* area. Similarly no food can contain any nonvegetarian element other than milk and its derivatives.

Since this is primarily a family or household *puja*, an area in the house is designated. A small altar can be made in the *puja* area so that it appears distinct. The other alternative is to have a wooden stool or a big metal plate, which should be washed with water and then placed on the floor. A *mandala* design can be made by using wheat flour or red powder on the surface of the stool. The plate is usually circular, hence a *mandala* (which means "circle") is not necessary.

It is most important to have Narayana or Vishnu seated in the center of the altar or the *mandala* design. Non-iconic forms of the images are used because these deities will be bathed. Vishnu's non-iconic form is a fossil stone called *shalagrama* or *shaligrama*. A silver coin: for example, a rupee, is also a symbol for Vishnu. Ganesha can be represented by a betelnut.

Other symbolic seats can be used in place of a *mandala*, for example, a drawing of a lotus-shape seating with eight petals *(ashta-dala-kamala)*. In the center of the lotus is the seat of Vishnu. For Ganesha, a *svastika* is drawn. The images of other deities are not necessary; hence, seats for them are not needed. Symbolically, all the deities, including the "house deity" *(Vastoshpati)* are seated in a vessel.

Other symbols or diagrams are drawn in which the respective deities are imagined as seated after they are invoked. For example, Shiva can be represented by drawing his trident. For the sixteen holiest "Mothers," a small rectangular area divided by four vertical and four horizontal lines provides sixteen spaces or "seats." Similarly nine spaces or seats would be drawn for the nine planets.

Such drawings are made with colors or wheat flour (or other flour) on a big plate or on the surface of the *puja* stool. The deities can be placed on the surface even without such drawings, as well as without any images or symbols; that is, images and seats are imagined to be there. The seat for the priest is on a small mat or rug placed on the south side of the central deity. The priest faces north or east. The worshipper sits on the west and faces toward the deities.

The following other items or materials are placed in the *puja* place within reach of the worshipper: a water pot, a sacred thread, red powder, sandal paste, turmeric paste, incense, rice grains, clarified butter *(ghee),* a sweet drink, sesame seeds, fresh fruits, fresh flowers and leaves, two small pieces of new cloth, a conch, a bell, a fire pot, small pieces of firewood or charcoal, a towel or a few napkins, betelnut, betel leaves, an oil lamp with clarified butter and a cotton wick, camphor pieces on a plate, and two spoons. If all of these items are not available, the essentials are considered to be a water pot, rice grains, scented paste of turmeric or sandal, incense, lamp, flowers, and the sacred food.

PURIFICATION AND INAUGURATION

Now the priest and the worshipper are ready to start the Worship. In their designated seats, they start purifying themselves and the surroundings. First the priest does a *pranayama* or breath regulatory exercise for which there are many techniques. A simple one is to sit erect and take the right hand to the nose. Close the right nostril with the thumb and breathe through the left nostril as gently as possible; then close it with the two fingers in the middle to hold the air as comfortably as possible, releasing the air through the right nostril slowly. Breathe the same way through the right nostril. That is: quickly close the left nostril, breathe in through the right, hold the air and release it through the left nostril. That is considered one cycle. Three such cycles are required. This *pranayama* in Hatha Yoga is called *nadi-shodhana* or Nadi purification, as it helps nerves, arteries, and veins *(nadis)*.

Then comes *achamana* "water sipping." The priest spoons up water from a pot and drops it on the cup-shaped palm of the worshipper. The priest says "*Om Visnuh*" and the worshipper sips the water. This is done three times. The fourth time the priest drops water again on the worshipper's palm, and this time the worshipper drops the water on the floor, preferably in an empty pot.

The priest then does *abhisheka* "shower, irrigation" by using a leaf or a spoon to sprinkle some water over himself, the worshipper, and all around, in order to purify the *puja* area, the audience and all the items. The following mantra, remembering Vishnu who has lotus-like eyes, is also said:

Pure or impure, or in whatever state one is, should
he remember the Lotus-eyed he is clean in and out.

It is assumed here that the priest and the worshipper already took baths some time before the *puja* for their external purity. The priest puts on a fresh, clean, white *dhoti,* a five or six-yard unsewn cotton cloth wrapped around the waist and below. A clean shirt called *kurta* is an optional upper garment for the priest. The worshipper also should put on clean clothes. Internal purity is achieved by the breathing exercise, which is not necessary for the worshipper.

Of much more import to the worshipper is to fast from morning to the end of the *puja*. The fast, called *upavasa,* varies according to the condition of the worshipper. Should he or she feel weakness, fruits or any non-intoxicating drinks (including water) are allowed in the fast. For other participants the same cleanliness rules apply, but only optionally. The name of Vishnu, who has beautiful eyes like lotuses (*Pundarikaksha),* is enough to make them pure inside and outside. Additionally the drops of water from the sprinkling fall on them. These drops are symbolically the waters of Narayana's cosmic sea from whence came Brahma, the Creator, on a lotus. Thus, a pure or fresh life is suggested here by this sprinkling.

Since all seats have their bases on the earth, it is customary to honor Prithivi, the goddess of Earth with the following mantra:

Om. Earth! All the quarters are held upon you.
Goddess, you are held by Vishnu. Goddess, you
hold me, and my seat pure.

With its recitation the priest sprinkles water around the floor and on his and the worshippers' seats. The small lamp containing *ghee* or clarified butter and a cotton wick is lit and placed to the left or in front of the main deity, with the following mantra:

O lamp! You are the form of Brahman, dispeller
of darkness. Accept the worship done by me,
increase the radiance.

The following salutation to the lamp is uttered with hands folded as in
prayer:

Om. Salutation to the enlightener.

This salutation is based on a general formula for honoring any sacred entity.
The noun for the entity is put in its grammatical dative form with the sacred
syllable *Om* in the beginning and a salutatory word *namah* at the end. Thus
the above salutation is as follows:

Om dīpāya namah
(Om to-the-lamp salutation)

Now the priest and the worshipper place a *tilaka* mark on each other's
forehead as the priest recites the following mantra:

May there be well-being and may there be good.
May the great Lakshmi be pleased. May all gods
protect you. Prosperity! Be well established.

The *tilaka* or *tilak,* made with saffron or vermilion or turmeric, symbolizes
here the blessing of Lakshmi, goddess of prosperity. It also implies that the
worshipper accepts the priest as the authorized official of the entire
ceremony. Now the priest is called *purohita* "priest," and the worshipper
yajamana "ceremony performer, worshipper."

To declare that the performance of the *puja* is about to begin, the priest
blows the conch and rings the bell. Whenever the conch is blown, people
from the audience, with or without the worshipper, say loudly in their
language:

Victory to Lord Satya Narayana!

THE AUSPICIOUS RECITATION

Now the priest recites the mantras for *svasti-vachana* (*svasti* "well-being," *vachana* "uttering, recitation") in order to wish for the successful completion of the *puja*. The following Vedic mantras are commonly recited:

> May right judgments come to us from everywhere undamaged, unimpeded, and penetrating. May the gods be always unretreated, protecting us everyday for our progress.
>
> Indra who is renowned, Pushan who knows all, Tarkshya whose wheel's rim is undamaged and Brihaspati–may all these hold well-being to us.
>
> May the heavens be peaceful, the atmosphere peaceful, the earth peaceful, the waters peaceful, the herbs peaceful, the trees peaceful, all gods peaceful, Brahman peaceful, all peaceful, peace and peace only. May that peace be to me.

The following Puranic verses are also recited:

> O goddess Shivā who is auspicious for all good works, fulfiller of all needs, shelterer, consort of Shiva the three-eyed, Gauri, and Narayani! Salutations to you.
>
> There is never a misfortune in any of the works of those in whose heart is situated Lord Hari, the house of fortune.
>
> To Vinayaka, Guru, Sun, Brahma, Vishnu, Shiva, and Sarasvati I bow for success in all works.
>
> In all the works that have begun let the three lords of the three worlds, the gods Brahma, Shiva, and Vishnu direct success to us.

Here the mantras recognize major Vedic gods such as Brihaspati "the big Lord," Indra, Pushan "Nourisher," Tarkshya or *Garuda* "the Eagle," etc. The big five deities, the trinity of Vishnu, Brahma, and Shiva, and Sarasvati as well are recognized in the verses.

TAKING THE VOW

Now comes the time for the worshipper to take the vow or commitment (*samkalpa*). He places sesame seeds or white rice grains with water in his right hand. The priest can use the simple vow given earlier, or a more elaborate vow given below in an abridged form:

> Today on the current Brahma's day in the second half of the "white boar" kalpa of the Vaivasvata Manu period, in the first quarter of the Kali yuga with the Buddha avatar, in this country, in this year's current month and this date I, born in such and such lineage with such and such name, shall perform for the sake of fulfilling all wishes the *puja* for Ganesha, Earth, Kalasha, nine planets, Satya Narayana, havana, etc.

Besides the name of the country, the worshipper adds the name of the region and the specific town or village. Similarly, the date includes the actual lunar day and the day of the week as well. The clan or "lineage" (*gotra*) in the Puranic sense is not always known to everyone. In such cases the *pandits* (pundits) suggest the use of "in Kashyapa's lineage" (*Kaśyapagotre*). In the Puranic view of creation, humans share sage Kashyapa as their common forefather. Note also that the current day, date, month, and year are placed within the cosmic time of Brahma, the Creator. In the simple vow given before, the worshipper can mention his or her family name instead of the lineage, followed by his or her own name.

The *pujas* listed in the elaborate vow are more or less the same except that the earth worship and havana are clearly mentioned. All the minor *pujas* must be considered variables. Only two of the *pujas* are obligatory— The Ganesha *puja* and the Satya Narayana *puja*. But whatever minor *puja* or ceremony the worshipper or the priest includes in the vow has to be performed, even though very briefly.

As soon as the vow has been said, the worshipper drops the contents of his hand in front of the main deity, namely Vishnu.

THE ESTABLISHMENT

The deities to be worshipped have to be invited and established on their seats in the *puja* place. The icon or image is placed in the normally designated section as the seat of the deity. The icon or image is called *murti* which means "likeness," that is, the image or picture of the deity, not the deity himself or herself. The deity is invoked or invited to settle in the image and make it his or her "body *(vigraha);* in short, the image must become a live body of the deity, given that life *(prana)* with a ceremony or ritual called "life establishment" *(prana-pratishtha).*

There are two kinds of establishments, one temporary, called *chala-pratishtha* "movable establishment"; the other permanent, called *achala-pratishtha* "immovable establishment." In homes the deities to be worshipped are dealt with by invitation, *avahana* and farewell, *visarjana.* That is, they come and go and hence are movable. In shrines or temples the deities are established only once, with a long and elaborate "life-establishment" ceremony after which the temple becomes the permanent home of the deity. The image or images are placed there with "immovable life establishment."

THE OFFERINGS

Now the deities have come in the house of the worshipper. In the *puja* they are guests, to be treated like kings or queens. Each deity in turn receives honor and hospitality for the worshipper in the form of offerings called *upachara* "service, means, conduct, offering." One can offer the guests a simple greeting with folded hands accompanied by a bow, or one can offer a seat, a drink, and food. The more elaborate occasion is a party to which relatives, friends, neighbors, and colleagues are invited in honor of the guests. Not only are the guests offered "services," but all persons attending share in the celebration. The party model (jokingly called the *"puja* party") is the most common.

In the Satya Narayana *puja*, the deities usually are honored with one of two sets of offerings, a set of five and one of sixteen. The set of five is called the *panchopachara (pancha* "five" and *upachara* "serving," or "offering"), and the five are a scent, a flower, an incense, a lamp, and a sweet food. The set of sixteen is called *shodashopachara.* In practice, the offerings vary according to the status and gender of the deity as well as the circumstances of the worship and the place where the worshipper lives.

The worshipper closes his or her eyes in meditation for a minute or so, then bows with folded hands to the deity. Then, as guided by the priest, he begins the offering with the "formula sentence":

"I offer X,"

where "X" stands for the particular offering. The formula sentence may or may not be preceded by an appropriate mantra.

The first offering after the invitation and seating is water for washing the feet of the guests. There is a small pot in front of the worshipper from which he picks up water with a spoon as he says the following formula sentence (or the priest says in his behalf):

"I offer padya."

In Sanskrit it is *pādyam samarpayāmi; pādyam* meaning the item "worthy of the feet," and *samarpayāmi* meaning "(I) offer." The item worthy of the feet here is the water that the worshipper drops at the feet of the icon or image of the deity. The next offering is water for the hands, and the formula sentence is:

"I offer arghya."

Arghya means the "item for honoring," in this case, water to wash the hands of the guest deities. The worshipper drops water on the hands of the images.

In a similar manner, these other offerings take place: *achamana* "sipping of water," *snana* "bath," *vastra* "clothes," *upavita* "sacred thread," *gandha* "scent," *akshata* "unbroken" rice or sesame seeds, *pushpa* "flowers," *dhupa* "incense," *dipa* "lamp," *naivedya* "present, food," *tambula* "betel leaf," *phala* "fruit," *nirajana* "waving of lights," *pradakshina* "circumambulation."

The *snana* or bath is of two kinds, one water and the other *panchamrita* (*pancha* "five" and *amrita* "ambrosia"). Actually, *panchamrita* is a drink (from the same word origin as English "punch," literally a drink with five ingredients). This drink is made of milk, yogurt, clarified butter, honey, and sugar. The *gandha* or scent is usually a paste of sandal or turmeric powder. The *akshatas* are usually mixed with *kunkuma* or *kumkuma*, a red powder of saffron, vermilion, etc., and wet with water.

The betel leaf can be replaced by *akshata* grains or seeds. The clothes and sacred thread can also be replaced by *akshatas*. The female deity is offered jewelry or vermilion instead of the sacred thread (only males can have the sacred thread or *upavita*). A small string made with yellow and red threads can replace clothes for male or female deities. For waving lights, camphor pieces can be replaced by cotton wicks soaked in clarified butter. They are lit on the plate, which is waved in a clockwise motion three times around the image. Circumambulation is moving around the deity toward the right (*pradakshina* "round to right"). In a shorter method, the worshipper stands up and moves in place toward his right hand circularly for three rounds. In the shortest method, the worshipper places a flower in his open right palm and moves it around the deity in the right direction three or five times. Turmeric powder mixed with lemon juice can replace the wet red *kumkuma*.

Whenever one material is substituted for another, the worshipper or the priest says something like the following; for example:

"I offer akshatas for betel leaf"

and then places the rice grains on the head (near the mouth) of the image. If it is a non-iconic symbol, then the materials for offering are placed or dropped on its topmost part.

It is clear that the *puja* offerings are based on the metaphor or model of "guest honoring." But the more subtle metaphorical sense is that one receives favors from the guests or deities. The favor is the fulfillment of one's own wish. The materials and their use in these offerings symbolize the process of germination and fructification of the wish. The wet red powder is the female (fertility) principle, and the white rice grains are the male (fecundity) principle. These two are mixed and offered to the deities who represent the environment or space. The use of water, lamp, and waving lights symbolizes the control of heat, cold, moisture, and so on. Other ingredients, such as milk and yogurt, symbolize nutrients for healthy growth of the wish plant. Finally, betel leaves, flowers, and fruits symbolize the blossoming of the wish.

THE GANESHA WORSHIP

Ganesha is the first deity to receive the first *puja* as he is the "lord of the attendants" or Ganapati. Here the attendants as well as the audience attending the *puja*, are his troops. His armies remove all the obstacles and lead the attendants to success or *siddhi*. The worshipper or the priest invokes him with Vedic mantras. A common invocation is as follows:

> I invoke you, the lord of attendants, the Ganapati.
> I invoke you, the lord of pleasures, the Priyapati.
> I invoke you, the lord of riches, the Nidhipati.

A set of non-Vedic verses is recited containing his twelve names: *Sumukha* "the beautiful-faced," *Ekadanta* "the single-toothed," *Kapila* "the tawny," *Gajakarnaka* " one who has elephant's ears," *Lambodara* "one who has a big belly," *Vikata* "the tough one," *Vighnanasha* "the destroyer of obstacles," *Vinayaka* "the best leader," *Dhumraketu* "the smoke-bannered," *Ganadhyaksha* "the head of the troops," *Bhalachandra* "one who has the moon on his forehead," and *Gajanana* "the elephant-faced."

These names describe Ganesha's features or functions; for example he is big-bellied or destroyer of difficulties, and so on. It is said at the end of the list of these names that whoever recites or hears them during the initiation of learning, marriage, housewarming, journey and war—in all those works no obstacle is born to him.

Then the worshipper offers him water for feet, hands, sipping, and so on, ending with a *namaskara* or salutation.

THE SACRED VESSEL

The Kalasha "jar, pitcher" is the water vessel. It usually contains five leaves (preferably mango) dipped partly in the water with tops up and tilted out. This serves several purposes: The major one being as all-inclusive or "cover-all" symbolic seat of all the deities. After its *puja*, the Kalasha's water is sprinkled around with a leaf to symbolize pure and peaceful environment. Part of the water can be transferred to another pot and used for water offerings: for feet, hands, sipping, etc.

In a more elaborate setting, the Kalasha is placed on a plate or a plain floor surface covered with various "seven grains" *(sapta-dhanya),* although rice is considered as an acceptable substitute for all grains. A coconut is placed on top of the Kalasha, and red or yellow thread is tied around the neck of the vessel or the coconut. The *akshata* and *kumkuma* (rice grains and the wet red powder) are placed together on the vessel's neck. All such symbols—grains or other seeds and powder at the bottom or neck of the vessel, water inside the vessel, and leaves and coconut on its top—signify fertilization of the worshipper's wish that at the end grows up, blossoms, and fructifies. Sometimes a *shalagrama,* instead of a coconut, is placed on the top of the vessel, and this non-iconic symbol is given offerings.

Other names for the Kalasha *puja* is the *puja* of Varuna, who in post-Vedic mythology rules over the waters or seas. The vessel is also identified as the pot of *amrita* or ambrosia that came out of the churning of the cosmic sea. The waters of this sea represented in the vessel are the symbolic source of life. The mantras or verses to be said in the Kalasha *puja* refer to Varuna, *amrita kumbha* or ambrosia pot, and life. The *puja* could be elaborate, but since Varuna has the status of a minor deity, a brief *puja* such as shown below is considered proper.

The worshipper touches the vessel with his right hand and invokes Varuna with a Vedic mantra such as:

> Then I came to you honoring with prayer as the worshipper praises you with offerings. O Varuna, arise here unangered. O widely praised one! May you not deprive me of life.

Then the Puranic *puja* contains the following:

> Salutation to Varuna in the Kalasha.

It is implied here that the worshipper does *namaskara* (with hands folded as in prayer) in front of the Kalasha. Then he or the priest places his right hand on the neck of the vessel and says the following verses:

> In the mouth of the Kalasha is Vishnu, in the neck is situated Rudra. At its bottom is seated Brahma; in the middle are remembered the groups of Mothers.

In the belly are all the seas and the earth with seven divisions; also the Rig Veda, the Yajur Veda, the Sama Veda, and the Atharva Veda.

And with their parts they all are situated in the Kalasha. Here is Gayatri, the Savitri, the peaceful, and nourisher.

May all these come to the worshipper as the destroyers of his sins. During the discourse of the gods and demons in the great sea when being churned,

You were born then, Kalasha! You were held by Vishnu himself. In your water are all the fords, all the gods are seated in you.

In you reside all the beings, in you are held the vital breaths. You are Shiva himself, you are Vishnu and Creator.

The Adityas, the Vasus, the Rudras, all gods with all forefathers—they all reside in you as they are the givers of the desired fruit.

With your grace I wish to perform this worship, O born of water! Bring your presence to me, Lord! Be pleased always.

Here those gods who are important but do not receive honor by separate *pujas* are included: for example, the eight Adityas, eight Vasus associated with Indra and Vishnu, and eight forms of Rudra or Shiva. It is impossible to name every deity, so all deities are believed to be established here. The worshipper now does an "all-inclusive" *namaskara* to them.

OTHER SHORT WORSHIPS

The group of nine planets (or *navagrahas)* is worshipped briefly. A vedic mantra or a Puranic *puja* verse can be used to invoke and praise each planet. The order of worship is as follows: Surya, Soma, Bhauma, Budha, Brihaspati, Shukra, Shani, Rahu, and Ketu. Most commonly, the following formula is followed in the planetary worship.

O Sun! Come here, sit here. Salutation to the Sun!

Akshatas mixed with *kumkuma* red powder are then dropped on the surface symbolically for the planet. Then comes another planet with the same *puja* format. The earth is worshipped with a mantra, but as a separate goddess.

In the end, a common prayer also is offered by the priest, such as the following:

> Brahma, Murari, Tripurari, Bhanu, Shashi, the Earth's Son, and Budha, Guru, Shukra, Shani, Rahu, and Ketu—may all these planets be peace-causers.

The names in this prayer respectively refer to Brahma, Vishnu, Shiva, Sun, Moon, Mars, Mercury, Jupiter, Venus, Saturn, Rahu, and Ketu.

The big five deities are also invoked and saluted with the formula shown above for the planets; e.g.:

> O Shiva! Come here, sit here. Salutation to Shiva.

Akshatas mixed with *kumkuma* are placed over the image or *linga* or on its surface. In this manner, Gauri, Vishnu, Surya, and Ganapati are honored. In fact, although Ganapati has already been honored, some gods are honored several times briefly. Vishnu, for example, comes here in the group; later he is worshipped as Narayana, the main deity of the entire *puja*. Gauri is included in the *puja* of *Matrika* or "Mothers." Lakshmi and Sarasvati are invoked separately as well as being included in the Mothers. The Lokapala or "world guardians" are then worshipped with the same formula.

One more small *puja* not mentioned in the vow, may be adopted by the priest. This is called the *vasordhara,* which literally means "streams of wealth." Seven vertical lines are drawn with warm clarified butter on the wall near the *puja* place. These lines symbolize the flow of riches into the house of the worshipper. Some hold that these are the seven out of eight Vasus, gods associated with Indra and Vishnu. But as "stream" or *dhara* is a feminine word, these lines refer to female deities; the salutation formula also addresses them as female deities, e.g.:

> Om. Salutation to the goddesses of riches.

After this salutation the worshipper may throw at them some *akshatas* and *kumkuma* to honor them. Other offerings, such as flowers, can also be thrown.

In the end the worshipper or the priest uses an all-inclusive or "cover-all" formula, as in the Kalasha *puja* also, to honor all deities with the following salutation:

> Salutation to all the deities.

Thus, in an easy and brief fashion all gods and goddesses are considered propitiated.

PRELIMINARIES TO THE MAIN SERVICE

After completing all the minor or supporting pujas, the worshipper and the priest focus their attention on the central deity, in this case Vishnu as Satya Narayana. First, the worshipper, required to meditate before Vishnu, holds one or more flowers in his or her hands folded as in prayer. The worshipper, with closed eyes, visualizes Vishnu, as described in the following verse:

> Meditate on the True; He is beyond qualities; He is the Master of the world and the ruler of the three worlds; He is Hari with his Kaustubha jewel. He has blue complexion, yellow garment, and is adorned with the mark of shrivatsa. He is Govinda, the joy of Gokula, and also worshipped by Brahma and others.

With this picture of Vishnu or Narayana in his or her head the worshipper opens his or her eyes after a minute or so and drops the flower near the deity. The worshipper now is prepared to honor the deity of meditation, namely Vishnu. The puja of the main deity is always longer than that of other deities, and one way to make it so is to use the sixteen Vedic as well as the Puranic offerings. Although the Vedic is optional, its addition is considered not only elaborate but also elegant.

For Vedic-style offerings the mantras of the *Purusha Sukta* or the "Purusha Hymn" are the most common. This hymn, occurring in the *Rig*

Veda (Hymn 90, Mandala 10), is basically a cosmogonic hymn that describes how Purusha ("Person, Proto-being") is the person who created the whole cosmos. This selection for the sixteen offerings is ideal as it has exactly sixteen mantras.

These mantras are used to honor any deity, such as Ganesha, or others, in any minor or major puja. But in this particular case it is even more proper to use them because Vishnu is identified as Purusha, the First Being (also *Adi Purusha* "First Person," *Purushottama* "The Person Ultimate," etc.), which this hymn is about. Vishnu means "Pervader" as he pervades everything. But the hymn says that "Purusha alone is this ALL." If such is the case, then not Vishnu only, but all other deities are covered by this "all-inclusive" concept.

It is not necessary to use all of the Purusha mantras; they can be combined partially or wholly with the Puranic offerings as is done when the Vedic offerings are used. A proper mantra from this hymn is recited, followed by a matching Puranic verse, and the offering is performed accordingly. The Vedic and Puranic versions will be given below, separately for clarity. The Puranic offerings are flexible too. There can be any number of them, but it will be seen that they are usually more than sixteen in the elaborate puja of the Satya Narayana.

THE VEDIC OFFERINGS

Below is a simple translation of the sixteen mantras of the *Purusha Sukta* from the *Rig Veda,* for the purpose of offerings. A mantra is recited and a matching dedication or presentation formula sentence is said, as pointed out earlier, with the name of the offering; for example, "I offer water for the feet" is the formula sentence for the offering named *padya* or "worthy of feet." Here only the name of the proper offering appears in parentheses after each mantra in order to imply the formula sentence. The original hymn does not contain any such parenthetical names or formula sentences.

1. Purusha had thousands of heads, thousands of eyes, and thousands of feet. He covered the earth everywhere, yet extended tens of digits beyond.   (*avahana* "invocation)

2. Purusha alone is this all, what has been, and what will be. He is the
   ruler of immortality, and of what grows by food.   (*asana* "seat")

3. Such is his greatness, and greater than this is Purusha. A quarter of him
   are all the beings. Three-quarters of him are the immortals in heaven.
                                                    (*padya* "water for feet")

4. With three quarters went up Purusha. A quarter of him here was born
   again. Then he spread over everywhere in animate and inanimate form.
                                                  (*arghya* "water for hands")

5. From that the Big Egg was born, from the Big Egg the evolved Purusha.
   Then born again he stretched over behind the earth as well as before it.
                                              (*achamana* "water for sipping")

6. When with Purusha as the oblation the gods performed a sacrifice,
   The spring was the clarified butter, the summer the fuel, the autumn the
   oblation.   (*snana* "bath")

7. That sacrificial Purusha, the one evolved ahead, they watered upon the
   grass. With him the gods, the Sadhyas, and the seers sacrificed.
                                                           (*vastra* "clothes")

8. From that wholly offered sacrifice was gathered the clotted butter.
   He made that the animals of the air, of the wilds, and of the village.
                                                (*upavita* "the sacred thread")

9. From that wholly offered sacrifice were born the Richas, the Samans,
   And the meters were born from that, and the Yajus were born from that.
                                                           (*gandha* "scent")

10. From that the horses were born and whoever are with two rows of teeth.
    Cattle were born from that. From that were born goats and sheep.
                                                          (*pushpa* "flowers")

11. When they apportioned the Purusha, how many ways did they partition him? What about his mouth? What about his two arms? What about his two thighs? What are his two feet called?　　　(*dhupa* "incense")

12. His mouth was the Brahmin, his two arms were made the Kshatriya. His two thighs the Vaishya; from his two feet was born the Shudra.
　　　　　　　　　　　　　　　　　　　　　(*dipa* "lamp")

13. The moon was born from his mind. From his eye the sun was born. From his mouth Indra and Agni, from his breath wind was born.
　　　　　　　　　　　　　(*naivedya* or *phala* "food or fruit")

14. From his navel there was the middle sphere; from his head the sky evolved. From his two feet the earth, the quarters from his ear; thus they formed the worlds.
　　　　　　　　(*pradakshina* or *tambula* "rounds or betel leaf")

15. Seven were his enclosing-sticks, thrice seven were the fire-sticks made, When the gods, extending the sacrifice, bound Purusha as the sacrificial animal.　　　(*nirajana* or *namaskara* "waving lights or a bow")

16. With the sacrifice the gods sacrificed the sacrifice. Those were the first laws. Those powers indeed reached the highest sphere where are the early Sadhyas, the gods.
　　　　　　　(*pradakshina* or *pushpanjali* "rounds or flowers")

The offering material or items may vary in their content or order. For example, the invocation may not be needed, in which case the third mantra would be employed for the *arghya* instead of the *padya* offering. With the "scent" the priest may add *akshatas* mixed with the *kumkuma*.

With these Vedic offerings it is implied here that a macrocosmic *yajna* or sacrifice is being represented here by a microcosmic *yajna*. This Purusha *yajna*, as it is called, is procreative. Because the worshipper's wish too has to be procreated, a small *yajna*, such as the Satya Narayana puja, is being performed.

THE PURANIC OFFERINGS

These are more important than the Vedic offerings, since this puja is basically Puranic. It is at the priest's discretion whether to combine these with the Vedic offerings. In the handbooks or manuals, the order and number of the Puranic offerings also vary from the Vedic. For example, the *arghya* verse precedes the *padya* verse, which means the water offering for the hands is performed before that for feet. Below the verse translation is followed by the offering in parentheses:

1. Salutation to the Lord of the senses whose form is manifest and unmanifest. Presented by me with devotion, let this arghya be accepted.
   (water for hands)
2. Narayana! Salutation be to you, the savior from the sea of hell. Accept padya, Lord of gods. Increase my happiness.   (water for feet)

3. This water, brought from all holy places is fragrant and pure. It is given to you by me. Please have it and sip it, Supreme Lord.
   (water for sipping)

4. Mixed with milk, yogurt, clarified butter, honey, and sugar also is this punch of ambrosia brought by me. Please accept it for bath.
   (a bath with the punch)

5. Better than all other ornaments, beautiful, remover of worldly shame, and prepared by me are these two garments for you. Please accept them.
   (clothes)

6. Made with nine threads and three strands is the godly sacred thread given to you by me.   (sacred thread)

7. This wood-rubbed sandal is divine, fragrant, and attractive. O best among the gods! Please accept the sandal paste as your makeup.
   (sandal or turmeric paste for makeup)

8. These whole grains, O best of gods, are beautiful as they are mixed with red kumkuma powder I have dedicated them to you with my devotion. Accept them, Supreme Being. (rice and red powder)

9. These flowers with fragrant mallika and malati jasmines have been brought by me for your worship. Please accept them. (flowers)

10. This top scent is produced from herbal extracts and filled with fragrance. This is the favorite incense of all gods. Please accept it.

(incense)

11. This lamp, filled with clarified butter, accompanied by a wick lit by me with fire is the destroyer of three worlds' darkness. Accept it, Lord of gods. (lamp)

12. The food for oblation is cooked with clarified butter; the milk pudding is with sugar. My naivedya is of many varieties. Please accept it, Vishnu! (sacred food)

13. This pure Ganges water is divine and destroyer of all sins. This is given by me as achamana. Please accept it, O First Purusha!

(water for mouth wash)

14. This betel leaf filled with cloves and camphor is honored by gods. Accept it with love, Lord of gods. Increase my happiness.

(betel leaf)

15. This fruit, God, has been placed by me in front of you. May gain of great fruits be mine in life after life. (fruits)

16. By this nirajana which is accompanied with four wicks and filled with clarified butter be pleased, Lord of the world! (waving lights)

17. The sins which have been committed in this and other lives, they all are destroyed at every rightward step. (circumambulation)

After the last offering the worshipper with flowers in his or her folded hands is ready to say the prayer. The verses for this purpose are translated below:

> Kindly accept the leaf, flower, fruit, water, and sweet food that I have presented to you with devotion.

> Sifter of people! Though short of mantras, short of activities and short of devotion my worship may be, let it be fulfilling for me, God!

> To Him who is unfailing, lotus-eyed, man-lion, destroyer of demons, lord of the senses, master of the world, lord of speech, giver of boons,

> To Narayana who is beyond from here I bow always with devotion. From difficult, odd, terrible, enemy-inflicted,

> And from all other undesirable fears liberate me. One must obtain the desired fruit having sung these names.

> I pray to Satya Narayana who is God, wish-giver and lord. Salutations to Him by whom the cosmos is fashioned for fun.

The major puja is over at this point when the worshipper drops flowers from his folded hands at the feet of the image, or near the deity symbol. Now the priest or the worshipper prepare for the most important part, which is the reading of the five chapters of the Story.

THE STORY READING

The five chapters that make the Story are believed to have been said first by Vyasa. As stated earlier, Vyasa is considered to be the greatest guru or teacher of the world. He must be honored as the Story opens with his name. A salutation may be said with the regular formula, such as:

> Om. Salutation to Vyasa.

Then the following popular verse in praise of the teacher is said:

The guru is Brahma, the guru is Vishnu, the guru is Lord Shiva the great god. The guru is the very Supreme Brahman, therefore, salutation to that great teacher.

After this, the priest turns his face toward the audience to begin the Story reading. He reads first in Sanskrit and then a translation in the regional language. Sometimes the Sanskrit version is not read at all. At the end of every chapter it is customary to say in chorus:

Victory to Lord Satya Narayana.

Such an utterance is indicative of the devotion of the audience. The priest or the worshipper at this time may blow the conch and ring the bell.

In this manner the five chapters are completed. The next step is to perform a *havana* or *homa* "fire oblation" ceremony.

FIRE OBLATIONS

The yajna in which food is burned for the deities is called *homa* "burned food." The other name for this ceremony is *havana,* which means food oblations to Agni, the fire god. The "pouring" is called *ahuti.* The basic ingredient poured is clarified butter (*ghrita* "ghee"). It is rich in fat; hence the ancient Indians considered it a symbol of a "topmost" food ingredient, and it must be offered to all the deities for their refreshment. More important is that the fat helps the wood burn faster. Other grains and materials can also be used with the clarified butter as well as without it.

For *havana* a fire pot called *havana patra* is commonly used in the puja area. Sometimes a fire pit called *havana kunda* is used instead. Small wood pieces called *samidh* are placed over the pot or pit. They are ignited with a mantra invoking Agni, the god of fire. Then the worshipper pours the clarified butter over the fire with a small ladle or spoon. The pourings correspond to the offerings that we here call "oblations," or *svaha.* This word is placed at the end of the name of the deity or entity for whom the oblation is intended. Thus, the formula sentence for the oblation is:

Om to X *svaha.*

The first oblation is for our first progenitor, Prajapati, later identified with Brahma. The worshipper pours one spoon of ghee or clarified butter for each deity that has been worshipped before; for example, Ganesha, Gauri, Shiva, the nine planets, the Mothers, etc. Theoretically all deities must receive this rich food oblation. So a "cover-all" or all-inclusive formula is said:

> *Om sarvebhyo devebhyah svāhā*
> Om. To all deities oblations.

Finally an oblation for the main deity, namely Satya Narayana, is poured with the following formula sentence:

> *Om Satyanārāyanāya svāhā*
> Om. To Satya Narayana svaha.

THE WAVING LIGHTS

Unlike the optional *havana* the grand light-waving ceremony is essential as the last act of pleasing the deity. In fact this ceremony is like a moving *havana*.

There are several names for this ceremony, such as *nirajana, artikya, arati,* and others. For this purpose, three or five cotton wicks soaked in clarified butter are placed on a metal plate. They are lit and the plate is moved three or more times up and down clockwise. In the last round the worshipper lowers the plate in a perpendicular motion and waves the light with his right palm toward the image. After the worshipper, the others may join. During the waving of lights, any prayer for Vishnu in any language can be sung in chorus by the audience, usually with folded hands. In Sanskrit there is a prayer in eight verses called *achyutashtaka* that starts with Vishnu's name and continues: Achyuta, Keshava, Rama, Narayana, Krishna, Damodara, Vasudeva, Hari, etc. For chorus use, prayers in modern languages are preferred. For example, a prayer in Hindi starts with these words:

Jaya Lakšmī ramana
Victory to Lakshmi's spouse.

This may be followed by another prayer that starts with the following line:

Om jaya Jagadīša Hare
Om. Victory to the Lord of the Universe, Hari.

Most major languages of India are very rich in devotional literature including the songs called *bhajana, bhajan,* etc. The word *bhajana* is related to the verb *bhaj,* as in *bhakti* "devotion." Singing of bhajans in chorus is called *kirtana.* It is not uncommon to sing bhajans in more than one language at this time.

While the prayer is sung, the plate with waving lights is carried around to each and every attendant in the audience. Every individual spreads his or her palms over the burning wicks in order to warm them, then places the warm palms on the forehead. This gesture symbolizes enlightenment of the devotee through God's grace, or burning the sins or sinful ideas of the devotee with the heat from God's light.

To express his or her gratitude for God's grace, the devotee can also put a monetary donation on a corner of the plate, which is usually quite large in expectation of such donations. Money collected through these donations is given to the priest or to any charity or temple. The priest receives it as part of his fees, called *dakshina* "donation, fee, cash gift," for priestly service. The worshipper actually gives *dakshina* after the puja is over or when the priest leaves the home.

FAREWELL TO DEITIES

When the prayer during the light-waving ceremony is over, the priest and the worshipper perform a "farewell" called *visarjana* for all the deities. The priest says the following Vedic mantra:

O gods, the knowers of the path! Having known the path, go on the path. Lord of the mind! O god! May this ceremony be auspicious. Place it in the air.

Usually the following Puranic verses are more common for farewell:

May all the deities, having accepted my puja, go away for fulfilling my wish and returning here again. (May all gods go to their places except Lakshmi, Kubera, and Sarasvati.)

(It is noteworthy that the three deities, Lakshmi, Kubera and Sarasvati may or may not be given farewell so I have put their mantra in parentheses.) Lakshmi is the goddess of prosperity, Kubera is the custodian of wealth (and a Lokapala "world guardian"), and Sarasvati is the goddess of learning. The entire puja is performed to increase prosperity, wealth, and learning. Thus, it is not considered practical to say good-bye to such symbols of power and prestige. All deities, however, are requested to return later again.

Satya Narayana is given a special farewell with the following verse:

Go, go the highest among the gods, to your place, O Supreme Lord, for the good of the worshipper, and come back.

All the farewell mantras or verses are said while standing in prayer position with folded hands (the worshipper and his or her family members standing beside the priest with folded hands also). Then a *namaskara* or bow is performed by these people, which, means in non-verbal communication "good-bye."

BEST WISHES AND BONDS

Now the priest places the wet red powder of *kumkuma* and the rice grains of *akshata* on the forehead of the worshipper (the *tilak* mark explained earlier) and a flower on his head. Then the priest picks up the coconut or any ripe fruit from the vessel and places it in the open palms of the worshipper with the following mantra:

May all the meanings of the mantras be fruitful. May all your wishes be fulfilled.

Here again are obvious these symbols of growing a wish in the body of the worshipper as a seed, flower, and fruit. At the same time this is the priest's way of wishing the worshipper the best. Moreover, the priest ties a sacred string made with red and yellow threads on the worshipper's wrist with the following mantra:

> By which the mighty demon king, Bali, was bound, with that I bind you. O Raksha! Don't move! Don't move!

The string is called *raksha sutra* "protection string, protective formula," and is tied on the right hand of a man or unmarried woman, but on the left hand of a married woman. This signifies the strong bond or ties needed for a happy relationship between the priest *(purohita)* and the worshipper *(yajamana)*.

The *tilak* is placed on others also, either by the priest or some volunteer from the audience; their wishes come true in the sense that the punch and the sacred food is served to everyone. This drink and food are called *prasad* *(prasada* "pleasure, grace"); it's the kind of sweet food (vegetarian with milk products) suggested in the first chapter of the Story. The worshipper receives the *prasad* after all others have received their share. Although the puja is considered over at this point, the worshipper and his or her family can provide a full vegetarian meal to everyone. This is a time considered good for more socialization in an atmosphere both happy and solemn.

A SIMPLER PUJA VERSION

The first chapter of the Story suggests a simpler style of Satya Narayana service than the one first presented. In practice the simpler style is far more popular than the priestly one. Once a priest is employed for this performance, it is obvious that Sanskrit and Sanskritic tradition will receive high priority. Since priests are not easily available, there is even more need to keep the service simpler. The simpler version of the Satya Narayana service is provided below only as an example of how people may become involved without a priest of Sanskritic tradition.

This version presumes inclusion of some basic items for the puja: fruits, the punch drink, vegetarian sweets, a lamp, incense, rice or sesame seeds, turmeric or the red *kunkum* vermilion powder, flowers, matches, a water pot, a metal plate, a towel or napkins, etc. A corner or section of the house is designated as the puja place, and washed with water, especially the portion where the items and images are to be placed. A wood stool or any small plate is used to place the images. An image can be replaced by its non-iconic symbol, such as a silver coin for Vishnu. The only image or symbol required is that of the main deity, Vishnu; his other avatar images or symbols, Krishna, a *shalagrama,* etc., are considered as good.

The worshipper needs a small mat or rug to sit on; it should be clean, preferably covered with a clean cloth or sheet. It is assumed here that the worshipper bathes before sitting for the puja and that he or she observes a fast all day until the puja is over. The fast may include any non-intoxicating drink, but water is considered the best. In case of extreme fatigue, any fruit can be eaten before the puja starts.

The worshipper and the audience sit without shoes in the puja area. The face of the worshipper is toward the east or the north or between the two directions. The worshipper then sprinkles some water from a pot over the images he or she is facing. A lamp is lighted and put in front of the images. Then the worshipper bows to them with folded hands in a prayer gesture; this is for a general invocation and welcome of the deities. Incense is burned at this time and put to the side. Then some rice grains mixed with the red powder or turmeric are dropped over the images, followed by flowers, and fruits and freshly cooked sweets are placed in front of the images as a symbolic presentation of all the offerings, to be followed by a *namaskara* bow with hands folded in prayer.

The most important part is the reading of the Story in translation. There are handbooks or manuals of the Story that contain translations in any major modern language of India, and the Story can be read by any person in the audience, including the worshipper. At the end of the Story all say in their own language:

Victory to Lord Satya Narayana.

Now the people can sing *bhajans* (devotional songs) in any language. Sometimes musical tapes or records containing devotional songs are also played. In fact, there are cassettes that contain the whole Story and the music that goes along with it. But most people prefer live performance of the Worship and the Story.

After a few *bhajans* comes the time for *arati* or the ceremony of the grand waving lights. A large metal plate with camphor pieces or ghee-soaked cotton wicks is used for this purpose. They are lighted and moved up and down around the image or symbol of the deity. The worshipper or any other person starts the waving lights. When this ceremony takes place all stand and sing the *arati* songs in their own language.

When the songs are over, the plate with burning wicks is passed around to every person. As said before, the waving lights are like the moving *havana* in which every person offers oblations to God in a symbolic manner. Such symbolism is suggested when each person moves his or her palms clockwise up and down over the flames twice or thrice, placing them over the forehead to receive God's grace.

The *prasad* consisting of food and drink that was offered in the puja is distributed among the audience as God's grace. The worshipper and his or her family may provide also a full vegetarian meal to all. The meal's quantity and quality vary according to the worshipper's circumstances. But it is only the *prasad* food that counts.

The *prasad* is basically a symbol of God's favor. It signifies pleasure, favor, calmness, tranquility, etc. It is so important that some people who may not be able to attend the puja or any other worship, in part or whole, will still make it a point to receive the *prasad*. Receiving it, no matter how much, removes their *avasad* or *avasada,* which means "sinking down, sadness, depression." The logic that works under *bhakti* is: If *avasad,* then *prasad.* Thus, *avasad* and *prasad* are not only related linguistically but also psychologically. One wants to feel up when he is feeling down and depressed. So we could say that it is the *prasad* that keeps the puja alive (or jokingly "No *prasad,* no Hinduism").

Prasad, however, is not necessarily a "food"; it could be just rice grains or flowers used in the puja. Important to note here is that in any version of the Satya Narayana *vrata,* the *prasad* is definitely food.

In the simpler version we observe no need of Sanskrit; it is really a short folk version of the Sanskritic type. There are smaller versions that include Sanskrit in a formula style. One sample of this will be provided in Appendix C.

It should be added here that many times an offering cannot be expressed overtly. Overt expression means that an activity is being performed in such a way that it can be observed objectively. For example, the worshipper gets up and goes around the image of the deity in order to perform the offering of "circumambulation." This can be observed because the activity is

expressed here physically or materially. But if the worshipper cannot offer
any physical expression of circumambulation, then he or she can "imagine,"
while sitting in one place, that he or she is going around the deity image.
In fact, all the offerings can be completed by creating such imaginary
situations. A puja done with such imaging of the activities and items
involved in the offerings is called *manasi puja* "mental worship," i.e.,
internal worship.

In an internal puja all the activities and items are imagined instead of
having real objects or words; no word is uttered, and no object is used. In
the Satya Narayana puja, the entire performance is not allowed to be done
in the imagination. But any offerings for which no items or materials are
available can be imagined. This way the puja becomes simpler, faster,
easier, and more economical. It is considered complete and even more pure
and honest because it is done without any "show." In any case, a puja
version based on imaginary offerings has to be the simplest, but then it loses
its ritualistic character, for a ritual is an expression or performance that can
be observed. The Satya Narayana Vrata or Puja is basically a ritual and
therefore must be expressive or overt, in part if not as a whole.

In actual practice some offerings take place internally only; some are
expressed verbally as well as materially. Verbal or linguistic expression of
an offering may be complete or incomplete. For example, the worshipper
could say *padyam* only instead of *pādyam samarpayāmi* "I offer (water) for
feet." Similarly, a material expression of an offering could be incomplete.
The worshipper, for example, may use the red powder without the rice
grains, while imagining or saying that he is offering the rice grains also.
These incompletions, however, are not considered flaws, partly because in
the *bhakti* religion formalities do not count, and partly because internal or
imaginary offerings are treated as genuine as the expressed ones.

Conclusion

Why should we seek to learn and perform the Satya Narayana Vrata Katha?

Performing any ritual means doing certain activities in succession or in sequence. Does the sequence make sense, or is it worthwhile? One answer is that any sequence, almost by definition "makes sense." Another is that a large number of human activities boil down to a question of survival. One of our questions, then, might be: How are the Satya Narayana ritual's activities related to survival?

As we reflect, for example, on the first chapter of the Story, we see that it deals with unhappiness, obviously the problem of humankind in all ages. In the Story, Narada is concerned with improving the quality of life. His question is: By what means could we bring about the destruction of human pain? A contemplative being, he looks for intuitive flashes as he engages in a monologue that is actually presented as dialogue between Narada and Vishnu.

This dialogue prescribes a set of activities for human beings to perform in order to have the good things of life. The set is as prescriptive as it is purposive, its purpose implied in these statements of the first chapter: "[This vrata] calms pain, sorrow, etc...increases wealth and prosperity; it produces good fortune and offspring and gives victory everywhere."

The attitude of the worshipper becomes more important as we continue to read. He or she on any given day must do this *vrata* with *bhakti* (which can mean sharing as well as devotion), and *shraddha,* which means faith. The *vrata* must include members of the family and community with the provision of food in the form of *prasad* for all. Traditionally the food must be one-quarter more than is needed for the invited guests; some strangers may show up and must be treated just like the guests. In the puja, the conch is blown intermittently, attracting the attention of the entire neighborhood with a sound as loud as an army bugle.

The concept of "sharing" is here expanded. The success of the *bhakti* religion results from the strong, symbiotic relationship between the literal

101

and metaphoric sense of sharing and devotion.   The tales reflect this relationship.

The pathway of the *Satya Narayana Vrata Katha* is wholly directed toward sharing through a devotional approach, considered to be in the interest of the individual as well as of the society. Performance of the ritual serves to identify the worshipper for his family and community, his friends, his colleagues, and, to a degree, even for strangers. Strong bonds are felt among the worshipper and his family during performance. Beyond this there is community bonding among neighbors and colleagues who solicit each others' cooperation and good will in the tranquil and sacred environment of the ceremony.

Hard feelings are often mellowed at this time. Even individuals not in speaking terms now may share something through the ritual: *prasad,* songs, or the passing of waving lights. Reading and hearing the Story together, participants realize the application to their own lives of the episodes in the Story where socially painful relationships are healed by the sharing of *prasad.*

Contact of various sorts among human beings, then, is an important component of success in the Worship–contact in a spirit of cooperation, and with attitudes of equality, empathy, hospitality, and sharing. Also of the greatest significance is the use of language: words as a symbol and expression of concepts or wishes or desires, combined with the materials used in the Worship.

A word also about the Worship with relation to Time and Space, which constitute the great support system for all human activities. The hospitality, even to strangers, the blowing of the conch to spread the news–all signify the desire to extend spatially the spirit of the Worship as much as possible. With respect to Time, a central aid of Worship from a mythological perspective is a desire for the "sure and soon" realization of wishes and desires within a single lifetime. Despite the philosophical ideas of karma and rebirth, this element of practical Hinduism is implicit in the Worship. One cannot wait for "slow" or cosmic (Brahmic) time or even for the "normal" human interval of time in which the "commitment" *(sankalpa)* is made by the worshipper. The material and linguistic expressions of the "offerings" in the ceremony ritualize the fertilization and fructification of the worshippers' wishes in "fast" time.

Hindus, like their fellow human beings, are concerned above all with betterment of the present life. The idea of achieving one's aims in "fast" time seems to have its roots in time as it functions in two phenomena: imaging and dreaming. In the fraction of a second, through imaging (as in a camera shot) a situation is formed. Linguistic expression, being linear, is somewhat slower. Material expression is slower yet—as the expression goes, "easier said than done." What the world has called "miracles" have been reported as the achieving of a material objective within the time of imaging.

The relationship of dreams to every day life is similar to the relationship of imaging to material expression. We are told that complex dreams can take place in an instant, whereas in reality what occurred in the dreams can take hours, days, or weeks.

To return to the subject of the Worship, the very power of God is sought in fulfilling a wish. As in a dream, God is imaged, showing compassion and power. Such an image is found in the material and linguistic expressions of theistic religions. In Hinduism Vishnu is manifested not only linguistically, as in prayers or mantras, but also materially as in his icons.

A typical icon of Vishnu shows his face as compassionate and tranquil also, suggesting that he is a sympathetic listener. He has extraordinary power as symbolized by his four arms. He can create, as shown by a lotus in one hand. He can destroy obstacles, as shown by a disc and a mace in two other hands. He makes everyone alert, active, and productive as shown by a conch in another hand. His human likeness elicits empathy as well as a personal relationship with the human devotee.

Having formed such an image of Vishnu, the devotees hope that the Lord will have a good image of them. After all, the mutual relationships of human beings are generated by the images they form of one another. If an employee forms a good image of the person in charge, and vice versa, there may be an opportunity for promotion or a quick raise in pay. This simple principle of image-worship underlies the honoring of icons in the Hindu puja.

In practice, the principle extends to "social image worship"; that is, people struggling to improve their images. A key to good social image-building lies in the proper selection and sequencing of activities. In the Satya Narayana puja the worshipper and his or her family find an opportunity to build or rebuild their images among the attendants who are members of the community: friends, colleagues, and—as we have shown—even strangers. Devotion to the deity is translated into honoring these members. Here each fellow human replaces the human image of the deity when consumption of the sacred food takes place at the end of the worship. The attendants attempt also to build or rebuild their respective images for the worshipper and members of family.

Continuous rebuilding of one's social image is perhaps equivalent to continuous reincarnation, aspiring to final "social moksha." The worshippers reborn in the stories have had to rebuild a social image by cooperation and altruism. For example, Moradhvaja was willing to sacrifice his own life to save a boy. Guha shared Rama's plight, even though the two characters came from different ethnic backgrounds. As represented by these episodes and others, the Story suggests that altruism is one of life's most desired ends.

Appendix A

PRONUNCIATION GUIDE

The Sanskrit language is written in the script known as "Devanagari" or "Nagari" (*Nāgarī*). An international convention adopted by linguists uses the Nagari script in the romanized version, which, however, must be interpreted for the convenience of the English readers. This version, it should be noticed, does not differ greatly from the English in which Sanskrit words have been presented in this book.

The following general statements approximate the pronunciation of those sounds; that is, the vowels and consonants, which differ considerably from English. Italics will be used to refer to the Nagari form of a Sanskrit term or word in this Appendix. In the Glossary, also, an italicized form appears after the gloss when there is a difference in the transcription.

The following statements should be helpful:

1. The Sanskrit vowels are either short or long and sometimes occur in combinations known as "diphthongs." The long vowel is shown by a macron or line above it. Thus *a* is short and *ā* is long, in the word *kathā* "story."
2. The underdotted *r* and *l* are treated as vowels, with short and long differences. Thus "Rig Veda" is *Ṛg Veda*.
3. The underdotted letters *t, th, d, dh, n, r* and *s* are retroflex sounds, meaning that the tongue is "retroflected" or curled back in pronunciation. Thus, "hatha" as in "Hatha Yoga" is *haṭha*, and "Pandit" is *paṇḍita*.
4. Consonants followed by *h* indicate more release of air in their pronunciation; hence they are called the "aspirated" sounds. These are *kh, gh, ch, jh, ṭh, ḍh, th, dh, ph*, and *bh*. Thus, the *kh* in *sukha* "pleasure" is closer to the *k* in the English word, "kill." However, the unaspirated sounds such as *k* in *karma* are like the *k* in the English word, "skill."
5. The undotted *t, th, d, dh* are called "dental." Examples are "t" and "d" in Latinic languages. The *th* in *kathā* is dental (as constrated to the *th* of *haṭha*).

The following list of most Sanskrit sounds, arranged in English alphabetical order offers an approximate pronunciation:

<u>Sanskrit sounds</u>	<u>English equivalents</u>	<u>Sanskrit words</u>
a	*u* in 'shut'	*satya*
ā	*a* in 'hard'	*māyā*
ai	*ai* in 'aisle'	*naivedya*
au	*ow* in 'now'	*Gaurī*
bh	*bh* in 'subhuman'	*bhakti*
c	*ch* in 'discharge'	*pañca*
ch	*ch* in 'chin'	*chanda*
ḍ	*d* in 'cord'	*Garuda*
ḍh	*dh* in 'woodhawk'	*dhola*
e	*ey* in 'grey'	*Veda*
g	*g* in 'go'	*Govinda*
gh	*gh* in 'doghouse'	*laghu*
i	*i* in 'hill'	*Agni*
ī	*i* in 'marine'	*Gītā*
k	*k* in 'skill'	*kāma*
kh	*k* in 'kill'	*sukha*
o	*o* in 'no'	*Soma*
p	*p* in 'spill'	*pañca*
ph	*p* in 'pill'	*phala*
ṛ	*ri* or *er* in 'river'	*amrta*
š	*sh* in 'shine'	*šānti*
ṣ	*sh* in 'mushroom'	*Krsna*
ṭ	*t* in 'port'	*Vikāta*
ṭh	*t* in 'torque'	*Hatha*
u	*u* in 'full'	*sukha*
ū	*u* in 'rule'	*Sūrya*
v	*w* in 'wait'	*Veda*

Note: The full mantras and sentences from Sanskrit or other Indian languages appear in italics in the book to indicate their romanized transcription and actual pronunciation as suggested in this Appendix.

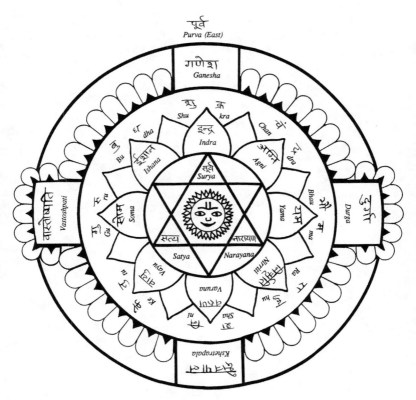

A Satya Narayana Mandala

Appendix B

A MANDALA AND THE PICTURE ON THE

FRONT OF THE BOOK

As indicated in the book, the use of mandalas is common in the tantric practices. Despite the attempt of Puranic Hinduism to avoid the influence of the tantras, a mandala like the one on the previous page may be used in the Satya Narayana worship. A typical tantric mandala contains mystical syllables called "bijakshara" (*bija* 'seed' and *akshara* 'syllable). Such syllables are *hum,phat, lam, aim, kraum*, etc. Numerals and mantras are used also as prescribed by tantric convention. The Satya Narayana mandala does not have such tantric features. It may have abbreviatory syllables, in which case the first syllable of the deity name is used. In the mandala shown, I have used all names in full, plus their romanization.

This mandala encloses a multi-petalled lotus, which is also a symbol of creation or Brahma. Around and inside the petals are seats arranged for the world guardians and planets (Lokapalas and Grahas). The name of each planet in Sanskrit has syllables that are split on the two sides of the petal. The sun or *Surya*, however, is seated in the center of the lotus and is the nucleus. The central deity, therefore, is placed in the center. Satya Narayana is shown in the same area. This customary placement of Surya and Satya Narayana shows clearly that they are identified with one another, as the full name of Surya is also Surya Narayana. On the outer circle are seated the four deities: Ganesha in the east, Durga in the south, Vastoshpati in the north, and Kshetrapala in the west. It is interesting to note that Vastoshpati is the god of housing; his name literally means "house lord." Kshetrapala is the god of agriculture, as suggested by the words *kshetra* 'field' and *pala* 'protector.'

Note the following: This arrangement of deities does not necessarily indicate the order in which they are worshipped. For example, the *graha puja* or 'planetary worship' starts with the sun (Surya) not with the moon

109

(Chandra). This mandala is simplified but the actual one is highly decorated and colorful. Various colors of powder or paste are used to draw the lines. The place for the sun, for example, is shown in red. Other deities not shown in the mandala are represented in additional non-circular designs.

A mandala is also called a yantra 'geometrical composition.' This mandala is circular, hence a "chakra" or round, circle, wheel, or cycle. The circles of the mandala represent the cosmic expansion, which is governed by its forces, the deities. Narayana causes this expansion, as suggested by his place in the center. This is why Narayana is believed to be the first cause or first person 'Adi Purusha.' The cosmos keeps expanding until all is over. Placement of the deities of agriculture and housing in the outer circle represents nurture and cultural evolution. Ganesha sits here on the east to symbolize the first or top priority of human beings to remove all obstacles to further beneficial expansion. Placement of planets represents worshippers' respect for the environment and their desire to be benefitted by it.

Like the mandala, the picture on the front of the book and also at the beginning of text symbolizes creation and expansion. This is a picture commonly used in the puja. It includes Narayana, Lakshmi, Shesha, and Brahma. Narayana is presented here as Vishnu Anantashayin (*ananta* 'infinite' and *shayin* 'resting'). Beside Vishnu are his typical holdings: mace, disc, and conch. A fourth holding, the lotus, is shown in his hand. Lakshmi is the mystical power, the 'maya shakti,' from which comes all prosperity. The cosmic serpent is Narayana's bed for rest: hence called 'remainder' or Shesha but also 'endless' or Ananta; its many hoods or faces with fangs are forces that protect and witness creation.

Out of Vishnu's navel is born Brahma, the Creator, shown seated on a lotus with the stalk representing the umbilical cord. Lakshmi is shown assisting at the delivery of the child from the navel of her husband. This picture I have placed on the front of the book between two Sanskrit lines, which are shown below with compound words, separated by hyphens. The topline is as follows:

Šrī-satya-nārāyaṇa-vrata-kathā

The first word, *śrī*, is added to a name as an honorific term. This word, however, is Lakshmi's name, appearing before Satya Narayana in order to assign priority to prosperity, which is ruled by Lakshmi.

The bottom line is one of the most popular salutatory mantras and reads as:

> *Om Laksmī-nārāyanābhyām namah*
> 'Om. Salutation to Lakshmi and Narayana.

In the picture the word *Om* is shown by its symbol, not by its letters. Here also Lakshmi appears before Narayana in order to invoke the mystic, moving power that underlies Vishnu, the Active. After a long cosmic rest, Vishnu must be active again, so Lakshmi stimulates and moves his feet.

With this worship are associated several family values at the micro- as well as the macro-level. This mantra is said at the beginning of the Ganesha worship with other salutatory mantras for the various deities. One of these is the following:

> *Om mātr-pitr-carana-kamalābhyām namah*
> 'Om. Salutation to the feet-lotuses of mother and father.'

Symbolically, with the association of these two salutatory mantras, the worshipper identifies the cosmic parents, Lakshmi and Narayana, with the human parents. The association of the lotus with the feet of the human parents and the lotus seat of Brahma are symbolic of creation. In addition to the parental identity being established, the human value of bonding between parents and child is also evoked by the obvious humanity of the pictured parents and offspring.

The parents must expect their child not to be simply a future creator but also a disseminator of knowledge. So the first books, the Vedas, or 'knowledge,' are shown in the hand of Brahma, the child. Brahma symbolizes research and development. His story means 'creation with knowledge.' When he finds himself on the lotus seat, his first priority becomes to know the roots of lotus. His next priority is to develop his own world, Brahma's *Srishti*.

The Brahmic world needs tremendous intelligence and activity for its formulation. Brahma's four heads and hands suggest the much-needed extraordinary powers of brain and action. We–all of us and our universe–make up this Brahmic world; hence we are all one family, as is said in the ancient Sanskrit:

> *Vasudhaiva kutumbakam*
> 'The world alone is the family.'

The picture embodies the idea of our common source, even if, like Brahma, we have difficulty in comprehending this truth. Because of this difficulty we are forced to suggest the first cause of creation by such various "names" and "forms" (*'nama'* and *'rupa')* as *Om, Narayana*, mantras, formulas, prayers, images, pictures, designs, temples, and a host of other religious symbols. Everything inherits that ultimate creative entity. It is extended through Brahma and through him extended further. Because it enters all things it is called Vishnu, the pervader or pervading.

At the same time, Vishnu means 'that in whom all things enter.' One becomes many and many become one. This cyclic emerging and merging, *'srishti'* and *'pralaya'* is simply for the fun *'lila'* of Narayana, who alone is *Sat* 'Existent'; hence the name Satya Narayana.

Appendix C

A BRIEF PUJA VERSION

A clean area is designated for the puja. A deep plate or bowl is used to contain an image of Vishnu in its center. The image may be replaced by a symbol such as a silver coin. All other deities are imagined as seated in the puja place. A few drops of water are sprinkled around by the worshipper while saying three times the name of Vishnu:

Om Viṣṇuḥ, Viṣṇuḥ, Viṣṇuḥ

The worshipper then bows with folded hands to greet Ganesha while saying one of the following sentences:

Om Gaṇapataye namaḥ
Om Šrīganeśāya namaḥ
(Om. Salutation to Lord Ganesha)

This is followed by the greeting to all deities:

Om sarvebhyo devebhyo namo namaḥ
(Om. Salutation and salutation to all the deities)

After the all-inclusive greeting comes meditation. The worshipper closes his or her eyes and visualizes the image of Vishnu. Then, with hands folded in prayer, the worshipper remembers the "wish" he or she has and bows while uttering the following greeting:

Om Šrīsatyanārāyanāya namaḥ
(Om. Salutation to Lord Satya Narayana)

or

Om Satyadeva namaste
(Om. Satya Deva! Salutation to you)

Now the worshipper honors Satya Narayana with the smallest version of formal puja, which consists of five offerings or "panchopachara" (*pañca* 'five' and *upacāra* 'offering'). Any deity may be worshipped with these offerings, each of which is accompanied by a *mantra* or sentence and the items and procedures shown below:

(1) *Gandham samarpayāmi*
   (I offer the scent)

While saying this sentence the worshipper places the scent, consisting of vermilion or turmeric powder with rice grains on the forehead of the image or over the symbol.

(2) *Puspam samarpayāmi*
   (I offer the flower)

With this sentence, a flower is placed over the symbol or on the head of the image (the flower usually falls down, as do other items mentioned above, and this is considered normal).

(3) *Dhūpam samarpayāmi*
   (I offer the incense)

With this sentence, an incense stick is placed in front of the image or symbol.

(4) *Dīpam samarpayāmi*
   (I offer the lamp)

Now a lamp is placed in front of the image or symbol with this sentence:

(5) *Naivedyam samarpayāmi*
(I offer the sacred food)

With this sentence some sweet (vegetarian) food or a fruit is placed in front of the image or symbol.

Now the worshipper, being sure to remember his or her wish, bows with hands folded in prayer for a few seconds. Then five chapters of the Story Text are read (audibly) in any language by the worshipper or another person.

After the reading, the worshipper performs the waving light ritual known as *nīrājana* (also *ārātrika, āratī, ārtī*, etc.) with the following procedures:

Four small cotton wicks are soaked in clarified butter (ghee) on a metal plate and lit. The worshipper moves the plate up and down, clockwise, three times around the image or symbol of Vishnu. The fourth time the plate is lowered, and the flames are directed toward or waved in the direction of the image or symbol. The right palm is used to wave the light.

The worshipper then puts the plate aside and bows several times with hands folded in prayer–as if to say farewell to all the deities. The final bow is for Satya Narayana or Vishnu. The worshipper silently requests of the deities the fulfilment of his or her wish and the deities' return.

At this time, one person picks up the plate with the wicks still lit and carries it to every person present. Each person waves the flames with his or her own palms, toward the forehead, one or more times, as if receiving God's grace. Songs in praise of God can also be sung at this time in any language.

As the ceremony closes, each person is served with some sacred food as "prasad," that is, God's favor.

Glossary of Sanskrit Terms

abhisheka/*abhiseka:* shower, bathing the deity with water or other sacred
  fluids, sprinkling of water for purification

achala/*acala:* immovable

achamana/*ācamana:* water-sipping in a puja, a water offering to the deity

Achyuta/*Acyuta:* the 'unfallen', Vishnu's epithet

adhyaya/*adhyāya:* chapter

Adi Purusha/*Ādi Puruṣa:* the 'first person', proto-being, Vishnu's epithet

Aditi: the mother of gods, Kashyapa's wife

Aditya/*Āditya:* the eight sons of Aditi, a name for the Sun

advaita: non-duality, non-dualism, the Vedanta philosophy

Agni: fire, Vedic god

ahuti/*āhuti:* pouring of oblation

ajnana/*ajñāna:* non-knowledge, ignorance

akshara/*aksara:* syllable; lit. indestructible

akshata/*aksata:* unbroken seeds, usually rice grains, as an offering for the
  deity

Alvar/*Ālvār* (Tamil): The Vaishnava saint from the south of India

Amba/*Ambā:* mother, Mother Goddess

amrita/*amrta:* ambrosia, nectar, the immortalizing drink

Ananta: non-ending, endless, infinite; a name of the cosmic serpent,
  Shesha, who is Vishnu's bed

Anantashayin/*Anantaśāyin:* one who rests on the infinite, Vishnu

Angiras:*Aṅgiras:* a sage and Brahma's son

anushtubh/*anustubh:* a couplet verse

Aranyaka/*Āraṅyaka:* books attached to the Vedas

arati/*āratī* (Hindi): the waving light ceremony; also *ārtī* (Sanskrit *ārātrika)*

aratrika/*ārātrika:* the light waving ceremony for a deity

archana/*arcana:* worship, worshipping the deity

arghya: an offering of water, etc., for the deity's hands

Arjuna: the third Pandava brother and Krishna's friend (in the
    Mahabharata)
artha: meaning, sense, earning, purpose
ashrama/*āśrama:* a life stage, hermitage, resting place, retreat
ashta-dala-kamala/*astadalakamala:* lit. 'eight petal lotus', a mandala
    diagram in the shape of eight petals of a lotus used in a puja
Ashtadhyayi/*Astādhyāyī:* the ancient Sanskrit grammar by Panini, lit. the
    'eight-chapter' book
ashvamedha/*aśvamedha:* a horse-sacrifice ceremony in ancient India
Ashvin/*Āśvin:* the twin gods, sons of Samjna and Sun
Atharva Veda: a Vedic book
atman/*ātman/ātmā:* self
atma-nivedana/*ātma-nivedana:* self-presenting, surrendering to the deity
Atri: a sage and Brahma's son
avahana/*āvāhana:* invocation, invitation to a deity in a puja
avasada/*avasāda:* depression, sadness, also *avasād* or 'avasad'
avatara/*avatāra:* incarnation; also 'avatar'
Ayodhya/*Ayodhyā:* the city where Rama was born

Badarayana/*Bādarāyana:* Vyasa's name
Bala Rama/*Balarāma:* Krishna's elder brother and Vishnu's incarnation
Bali: a demon king
Bhadrashila/*Bhadraśīlā:* a river
Bhagavad Gita/*Bhagavadgītā:* the 'blessed song', the discourse between
    Arjuna and Krishna in the *Mahabharata*
Bhagavan/*Bhagavān:* God, the Blessed One
bhaj: the verb meaning 'share, serve, present, submit, grant, dedicate',
    etc.
bhajana: a devotional song; also 'bhajan'
bhakta: devotee
bhakti: devotion, sharing
bhakti rasa: the devotional joy
Bhalachandra/*Bhālacandra:* one who has the moon on his forehead;
    Ganesha's epithet
Bhanu/*Bhānu:* the Sun
Bharata: Rama's brother or Kaikeyi's son (in the *Ramayana);* an author of
    the *Natya Shastra*

Bhauma: the planet Mars and one of the planetary gods
bhava/*bhāva:* attitude, feeling
bheda: break-up, tearing, difference
Bhilla Guharaja/*Bhilla Guharāja:* a chief of the Nishadas
bija/*bīja:* seed
bijakshara/*bījāksara:* a seed syllable (with mystic meaning)
Brahma/*Brahmā:* the god of creation
brahmacharya/*brahmacarya:* the first of the four stages of life; early student life
Brahman: Absolute Self (in Vedantic non-dualistic philosophy)
Brahmana/*Brāhmana:* books attached to the Vedas, a Brahmin priest
Brahmanda/*Brahmānda:* Brahma's egg, cosmic creation
Brahma-nirvana/*Brahmanirvāna:* liberation of *ātman* into *Brahman*
Brihaspati/*Brhaspati:* lit. 'the big lord'; the planet Jupiter and one of the planetary gods; gods' teacher
Buddha: the founder of Buddhism, an avatar of Vishnu; lit. the enlightened
Buddhi: intellect; Ganesha's wife
Budha: the planet Mercury and one of the planetary gods

chakra/*cakra:* circle, cycle, wheel, round
chala/*cala:* moveable
chandana/*candana:* sandal
Chandra/*Candra:* the moon; the moon god
Chandraketu/*Candraketu:* a king
Charvaka/*Cārvaka:* a school of materialistic philosophy
Chaturthi/*caturthī:* the fourth day in a lunar month
Chhanda/*chanda:* metrics
Chhaya/*chāyā:* shadow; a wife of the Sun god

Daityasudana/*Daityasūdana:* (*daitya* 'demon' and *sūdana* 'slayer'); Krishna
Daksha/*Daksa:* a Prajapati and Sati's father
dakshina/*daksinā:* cash gift or a fee given to a priest
Damodara/*Dāmodara:* Krishna's epithet
dana/*dāna:* donation, charity, favor, gift
danda/*danda:* stick, staff, punishment, penalty
Dandin/*Dandin:* stick holder; monk with a staff; a renunciate

darshana/*darśana:* view, philosophy; the Darshana books
Dasharatha/*Daśaratha:* father of Rama (in the *Ramayana*)
dasya/*dāsya:* the service attitude, servitude, service, devotion of service, servicing the deity
Deva: god
Devarshi/*Devarsi:* lit. the 'devine sage'; Narada's title
Devi/*Devī:* female deity, Goddess, the Mother Goddess
dharma: duty, norm, code, law, fairness, righteousness, behavior
Dharma Sutra/*Dharmasūtra:* ancient books dealing with various ethical duties, laws etc.
Dhumraketu/*Dhūmraketu:* the 'smokebannered'; Ganesha's epithet
dhupa/*dhūpa:* incense as an offering for the deity
Dikpala/*Dikpāla:* a 'direction protector' deity
dipa/*dīpa:* lamp, enlightner
dipavali/*dīpāvali:* the festival of lights
Dravidi/*Drāvidī:* Dravidian
dukha: also duhkha; pain, misery
Durga/*Durgā:* Mother Goddess, Parvati; lit. the 'inaccessible, incomprehensible'
dvaita: duality, dualism
dvandva: dualities, opposites
Dvapara yuga: see yuga
Dvaraka/*Dvārakā:* the capital of Krishna on the western coast of India (spelled 'Dwaraka' also)

Ekadanta: the 'one-toothed'; Ganesha's epithet

Gajakarnaka/*Gajakarnaka:* one who has elephant's ears; Ganesha's epithet
Gajanana/*Gajānana:* the 'elephant faced'; Ganesha's epithet
Ganadhyaksha/*Ganādhyaksa:* the 'troop lord'; Ganesha's epithet
gandha: scent, a powder or paste offering for the deity
Ganesha/*Ganeśa:* son of Parvati and Shiva
Garuda/*Garuda:* an eagle who is Vishnu's vehicle
Gauri/*Gaurī:* lit. the 'white' goddess; Parvati, Shiva's wife
gayatri/*gāyatrī:* lit. 'singer-savior', a Vedic meter, a famous mantra
ghee/*ghī* (Hindi): clarified butter (Sanskrit *ghrta)*
ghrita/*ghrta:* clarified butter; ghee

Gita/*Gītā:* 'song'; the *Bhagavad Gita,* the philosophical discourse between Krishna and Arjuna in the *Mahabharata*

Gokula: the place of the cowherds, the village where Krishna lived in his early life

Gokulananda/*Gokulānanda:* Gokula's joy, Krishna

gotra: lineage, clan

Govinda: herdsman, cow-finder, body protector, Krishna

grihastha/*grhastha:* the second of the four stages of life, a householder

Grihya Sutra/*Grhyasutra:* the ancient books dealing with domestic rites, ceremonies, etc.

Guha: chief of the Nishada people who helped Rama (in the *Ramayana)*

guna/*guna:* strand, loop, quality

Gunatita/*Gunātīta:* beyond the gunas or qualities, God

guru: teacher

Hari: an epithet of Vishnu, especially for Krishna, one who removes sins

Hatha Yoga/*Hatha Yoga:* a branch of yoga

havana: the ceremony of 'fire oblation' for the deities invoked

hiranya garbha/*hiranyagarbha:* lit. 'golden womb', cosmic or Brahma's womb, hence Brahmanda or Brahma's egg

homa: a ceremony in which the burned food called *homa* is offered to the deities; also 'havana'

Indra: the king of gods

Ishana/*Īśāna:* a world guardian identified with Shiva

Ishvara/*Īśvara:* God

Janaki Vallabha/*Jānakīvallabha:* Sita's (Janaki's) beloved, Rama

jaya: victory

jivan-mukta/*jīvanmukta:* a person living while liberated from the life cycle

jivan-mukti/*Jīvanmukti:* live liberation; salvation achieved while living

jnana/*jñāna:* knowledge

Jyautish/*Jyautiṣ:* books dealing with stars, star science

Kaikeyi/*Kaikeyī:* Bharata's mother (in the *Ramayana)*

Kailasa/*Kailāsa:* a mountain in the Himalayas, Shiva's abode

kaivalya: independence, separation of self-identity from matter or nature

kalakuta/*kālakūta:* a deadly cosmic poison
Kalasha/*Kalaśa:* the sacred vessel
Kalavati/*Kalāvatī:* a woman
Kali/*Kālī:* the black goddess; the goddess of Time, Durga
Kali Yuga: the age of Kali or darkness, the last of the four 'ages'
Kalkin: the Vishnu incarnation to come in the age of Kali
kalp: form, imagine, plan (from the verb *klp)*
kalpa: a cosmic time unit, a Brahmic day
kama/*kāma:* desire, love
Kama Deva/*Kāmadeva:* the love god
Kamsa/*Kamsa:* the cruel king of Mathura whom Krishna killed
kanchana/*Kāñcana:* a city with the name *Kancanapura*
kanta/*kānta:* loving, spousal love, devotion of love
Kapila: the 'twany'; Ganesha's epithet
kar: do (from the verb *kr)*
karma: action, deed, cause-and-effect
karma yoga: the philosophy of selfless action
Kashi/*Kāśī:* an ancient name for the city Varanasi (also Benares, Banaras)
Kashyapa/*Kaśyapa:* a Prajapati
katha/*kathā:* story
Kaurava: the hundred brothers who are the cousins of the Pandavas in the
    Mahabharata
Kausalya/*Kausalyā:* Rama's mother (in the *Ramayana);* also *Kauśalyā*
kaustubha: name of a jewel put on by Vishnu
Keshava/*Keśava:* Krishna's name
Ketu: a demon who eclipses the sun
khanda/*khanda:* section, region, part, division
kirtana/*kīrtana:* devotional singing
Kratu: a sage and Brahma's son; (lit. 'work')
Krishna/*Krsna:* a hero of the *Mahabharata,* especially the *Gita;* an avatar
    of Vishnu
Krishna Dvaipayana/*Krsnadvaipayana:* Vyasa's name
Krita Yuga/*Krtayuga:* the perfect age; name of the first Yuga, also Satya
    Yuga
Kshatriya/*Kśatriya:* the class representing warriors, rulers, administrators,
    a person from this class
Kshetrapala/*Kśetrapāla:* lit. 'field protector'; the god of agriculture

Kshira Sagara/*Kṣirasāgara:* Milky Sea where Vishnu resides
Kubera: a world guardian god, custodian of wealth
kumkuma: a red power of saffron or vermilion ; also *kumkum* or *kunkum*
kunda/*kunḍa:* pit
Kurma/*Kūrma:* turtle, the Tortoise incarnation of Vishnu

Lakshmana/*Lakṣmana:* Rama's brother (in the *Ramayana)*
Lakshmi/*Lakṣmī:* the goddess of prosperity, Vishnu's consort
Lambodara: big bellied; Ganesha's epithet
lila/*līlā:* sport, game, play, fun
Lilavati/*Līlāvatī:* a woman
linga/*liṅga:* sign; a phallic-shaped symbol of Shiva
loka: world, space
Lokapala/*Lokapāla:* a 'world guardian' deity

Madhva: a saint and philosopher of bhakti and dualism
Mahabharata/*Mahābhārata:* the great epic about the Kauravas and
    Pandavas with Krishna and others
mahapralaya/*mahāpralaya:* mega-dissolution; see *pralaya*
Mahapurana/*Mahāpurāna:* any major Purana
Mahavira/*Mahāvīra:* a founder of Jainism; lit. the 'great hero'
mahayuga/*mahāyuga:* mega Yuga, a unit of time; see *Yuga*
Mahisha/*Mahiṣa:* a buffalo demon killed by Durga
malati/*mālatī:* a jasmine
mallika/*mallikā:* a jasmine
manasa/*mānasa:* mental (*manas* 'mind')
manasi puja/*mānasīpūjā:* mental worship
manava/*mānava:* Manu's progeny, man, human
mandala/*mandala:* circle, round, collection, also 'chakra'
Manu Smriti/*Manusmrti:* the law book by Manu or Manu's laws
manvantara: Manu's interval, a time period of Manu
marga/*mārga:* way, path
Marichi/*Marīci:* a sage and Brahma's son
Mathura: the city where Krishna was born
Matrika/*Mātrkā:* mother, the holy mother deities worshipped as a group
Matsya: fish, the Fish incarnation of Vishnu
modaka: a small ball-shaped sweet

Mohini/*Mohinī:* the 'enchantress', a woman incarnation of Vishnu
moksha/*moksa:* release, salvation, relief
Moradhvaja: the king of Ratnapura and Krishna's devotee; also
    Mayūradhvaja
mukta: liberated
mukti: release, relief, salvation
Murari/*Murāri:* lit. Mura's enemy (*Murā* 'a demoness' + *ari* 'enemy');
    Vishnu's epithet
murti/*mūrti:* image, likeness, form, icon

nadi-shodhana/*nādī śodhana:* lit. 'fiber purifying'; a breathing exercise in
    yoga for removing the impurities of nerves, arteries, veins, etc.
Naimisha/*Naimisa:* name of a holy forest; also *Naimisāranya*
naivedya: sacred food as an offering for the deity
nama/*nāma:* name
namah/*namah:* salutation
namaskara/*namaskāra:* salutation; lit. *namas* 'bowing' + *kāra* 'act'
namaste: salutation to you (*namas* 'salutation' + *te* 'to you')
Nanda: foster father of Krishna
Nandin: the delightful, a bull who is Shiva's vehicle
nara: man, human, Narayana's brother Nara
Narada/*Nārada:* a sage and Brahma's son, Vishnu's devotee who learns
    first the Satya Narayana worship
Naradabhaktisutra/*Nāradabhaktisūtra:* a book with devotional aphorisms
    attributed to Narada, the famous sage
Narasimha/*Narasimha:* lit. 'man-lion'; the man-lion incarnation of Vishnu;
    also *Nrsimha*
Narayana/*Nārāyana:* God, Vishnu
Narayani/*Nārāyanī:* an epithet for Parvati, also for Lakshmi
nari/*nārī:* woman
nastika/*nāstika:* atheistic, non-theistic
Nayanar/*Nāyanār* (Tamil): the Shaiva saints from southern India
Nayta Shastra/*Nātyaśāstra:* Dramatic Science, a book attributed to Bharata
Nibandha: a group of books dealing with rites, rituals and sacraments
nirajana/*nīrājana:* waving of light as an offering for the deity
nirguna/*nirguna:* non-quality, non-form

Nirriti/*Nirrti:* a goddess worshipped by the demons and also a 'world guardian'
Nirukta: the etymology books in Sanskrit
Nishada/*Nisāda:* a tribe (in the *Ramayana)*
nishkama/*niskāma:* non-desire, desireless
Nyaya/*Nyāya:* a school of philosophy

Om: a sacred symbol or name of Brahman or God, a mantra, a syllable attached to a mantra in the beginning or at the end

pada-sevana/*pādasevana:* feet serving, serving the feet of the deity
Paddhati: a group of books dealing with rites, rituals and sacraments
padya/*pādya:* lit. 'worthy of feet'; an offering of water for the feet of the deity
panchamrita/*pañcāmrta: (pañca* 'five' + *amrta* 'ambrosia'); a sacred drink with five ingredients for offering to the deity
Pancharatra/*Pañcarātra:* a Vaishnava tradition, its books
panchopachara/*pañcopacāra: (pañca* 'five' + *upacāra* 'offering'); a set of five offerings for the deity
pandita/*pandita:* wise person, scholar, professional priest, Brahmin; also *pandit* 'pundit'
papa/*pāpa:* sin, bad karma
Parasharya/*Parāšarya:* Parashara's son, Vyasa, whose father's name is *Pārāšara*
Parashu Rama/*Parašurāma:* Rama with an ax; a Brahmin incarnation of Vishnu
Parvati/*Pārvatī:* the Mother Goddess; Shiva's consort, Durga
patra/*pātra:* pot
paurnamasi/*paurnamāsī:* the 'full moon' day
phala: fruit
Pitamaha/*Pitāmaha:* grandfather; Brahma's title, being the oldest creator
pradakshina/*pradaksina:* moving to the right, circumambulation
Prahlada/*Prahlāda:* a demon devotee of Vishnu, son of Hiranyakashipu
Prajapati/*Prajāpati: (prajā* 'progeny' + *pati* 'lord'); a god of creation in the Vedic mythology
pralaya: absorption, dissolution
prana/*prāna:* life force, vital breath

prana-pratishtha/*prāṇapratiṣthā:* the ceremony of 'life-establishment' in the image of a deity

pranayama/*prāṇāyāma:* the breathing exercises of yoga

prasad: same as prasada

prasada/*prasāda:* pleasure, sacred food, grace; also *prasād*

pratishtha/*pratiṣthā:* establishment

Prithivi/*Prithivī/Prthvī:* earth; the goddess Earth

puja/*pūjā:* worship, religious service, honoring a deity

Pulaha: a sage and Brahma's son

Pulastya: a sage and Brahma's son

Pundarikaksha/*Puṇḍarīkākṣa:* lit. the 'lotus-eyed'; Vishnu, whose eyes are beautiful like lotuses

punya/*puṇya:* good deed, merit of a good karma

Purana/*Purāṇa:* a work of classical mythology (lit. ancient book); the Puranas

purohita: priest, community's well-wisher (lit. 'front-situated', hence leader or guide)

Purusha/*Puruṣa:* Person, Proto-being, man, Vishnu's first incarnation

purushartha/*puruṣārtha:* person's purpose, the four goals known as dharma, artha, kama, and moksha

Purushottama/*Puruṣottama:* lit. the 'person ultimate'; the topmost man; Vishnu's epithet

Pushan/*Pūṣan:* lit. the 'nourisher'; a Vedic god

pushpa/*puṣpa:* flower

pushpanjali/*puṣpāñjali:* flower offering (*puṣpa* 'flower' + *añjali* 'offering given by hands')

Radha/*Rādhā:* a milkmaid who loved Krishna

Rahu/*Rāhu:* lit. the 'grabber'; a demon who eclipses the moon

Rajanya/*Rājanya:* the 'royal' class called 'Kshatriya'

rajas: a quality or *guna* of the second degree

raksha sutra/*rakṣāsūtra:* a 'protection string' put on the wrist

Rama/*Rāma:* the hero of the *Ramayana;* an avatar of Vishnu

ramana/*ramana:* the enjoyer, lover, enjoyment

Ramanuja/*Rāmānuja:* a saint and philosopher of bhakti and Vedanta

Ramayana/*Rāmāyaṇa:* the great epic about Rama

Ranganatha/*Raṅganātha:* Vishnu; the Vishnu temple in modern Srirangam (near Madras)

rasa: fluid, taste, esthetic enjoyment, emotion, joy, flavor

rasa-nishpatti/*rasa-niṣpatti:* emotional release, esthetic experience

rasayana/*rasāyana:* chemical, medicine

Rati: name of Kama Deva's wife, goddess of love; lit. 'sex, sexual act'

Ratnapuri/*Ratnapurī:* a city

ratri/*rātri:* night

Reva/*Revā:* a name for the Narmada river in central India

Revakhanda/*Revākhaṇḍa:* the section of the *Skanda Purana* in which the text of the Satya Narayana ritual is given

richa/*ṛcā:* verse, mantra from the *Rig Veda* (found before otherwords as *ṛc-, ṛg-, ṛk-, e.g. Ṛg Veda*)

Rig Veda/*Ṛg Veda:* the oldest Veda book

Rishi/*Ṛṣi:* seer, saint, wise

Romaharshana/*Romaharṣaṇa:* Suta's father

Rudra: lit. the 'fierce', Shiva's name; also the eight forms of Shiva known as the 'eight Rudras'

Rukmini/*Rukminī:* Krishna's wife

rupa/*rūpa:* form

Sachchidananda/*Saccidānanda:* Brahman or Vishnu with three aspects of *sat* 'existence', *cit* 'consciousness' and *ānanda* 'bliss'

saguna/*saguna:* with-form, with-quality

sakama/*sakāma:* with-desire

sakhya: friendly attitude, friendship, devotion of friendship, befriending the deity

salokya/*sālokya:* sharing the same place, living with the deity in a liberated state

sama: equal, equanimous in temper

samadhi/*samādhi:* the eighth stage in yoga, the stage beyond meditation

saman/*sāman:* the *Sama Veda* chants, settlement, concilliation, one of the four means in diplomacy

samarpayami/*samarpayāmi:* 'I offer'

Sama Veda/*Sāma Veda:* a Vedic book

Samidh: wood pieces used to light the fire in the 'homa' ceremony

samipya/*samīpya:* proximity, living close to the deity in the liberated state
Samjna/*Samjñā:* consciousness, a wife of the Sun
samkalpa/*samkalpa:* vow, commitment, decision, plan
Samkhya/*Sāṃkhya/Sāṅkhya:* a school of philisophy
samnyasa/*samnyāsa/sannyāsa:* renunciation, the fourth of the four stages
    of life
samsara/*samsāra:* creation, world, continuum of life or existence
Sanaka: a sage and Brahma's son
Sananda: a sage and Brahma's son
Sanatana/*Sanātana:* senior, ancient, everlasting, perpetuating; a son of
    Brahma
Sanatana Dharma/*Sanātanadharma:* the senior religion, the ancient
    tradition, the traditional Hinduism
Sanatkumara/*Sanatkumāra:* a son of Brahma
sandhya/*sandhyā:* a junctional prayer
sankalpa/*sankalpa:* same as samkalpa
sannidhya/*sānnidhya:* proximity, closeness to the deity in the liberated state
sapada/*sapāda:* one unit plus a quarter of it
sapta-dhanya/*saptadhānya:* seven grains, a combination of seven sacred
    grains used in the puja
Sarasvati/*Sarasvatī:* the goddess of learning and music, Brahma's daughter
sarupya/*sārupya:* sharing the form, looking like the deity in the liberated
    state
sat: true, truth, real, existent
Sati/*Satī:* Parvati in her previous life
sattva: a *guṇa* or quality of the highest (first) degree
satya: truth or true
Satyagraha/*satyāgraha:* (*satya* 'truth' + *āgraha* 'force'); Mahatma Gandhi's
    non-violent civil disobedience
Satyavatisuta/*Satyavatīsuta:* Satyavati's son, Vyasa, whose mother's name
    is *Satyavatī*
Satya Yuga: see yuga
Savarni/*Sāvarni:* a son of the Sun god
Savitar: stimulator,vivifier, impeller, the sun, the Sun god, also *Savitr*
Savitri/*Sāvitrī:* a name of Gayatri, related to *Savitr*
sayujya/*sāyujya:* sharing the union, meeting the deity in the liberated state
Shaiva/*Śaiva:* Shiva's devotees; Shaivism, belonging to Shiva

Shakta/*Śākta:* a Shakti or Mother Goddess devotee; belonging to Shakti; Shaktism

Shakti/*Śakti:* power, energy, force, the Mother Goddess

Shalagrama/*Śālagrāma:* a fossil stone used as a symbol of Vishnu

Shaligrama/*Śāligrāma:* same as Shalagrama

Shandilya/*Śāndilya:* a sage to whom a book of devotional aphorism, *Śāndilyasūtra,* is attributed

Shani/*Śani:* lit. 'slow mover'; a son of the Sun, Saturn

Shankara/*Śankara:* a Vedanta philosopher and monk; also Shankaracharya (*Śankarācārya*)

shanti/*śānti:* peace, tranquility, calm

Shashi/*Śaśi:* the Moon

Shatarupa/*Śatarūpā:* Brahma's daughter and Manu's wife; lit. a female with hundreds of forms

Shaunaka/*Śaunaka:* a sage who heads a group of rishis

Shesha/*Śeṣa:* lit. the 'remainder'; the cosmic serpent who is Vishnu's couch

Shiksha/*Śikṣā:* the books on phonetics

Shiva/*Śiva:* good, happy, auspicious; the god of cosmic dissolution; God; Parvati's spouse

Shiva/*Śivā:* Shiva's wife, i.e. Parvati (lit. the 'auspicious' Goddess)

shloka/*śloka:* a couplet verse

shodashopachara/*sodaśopacāra:* (*sodaśa* 'sixteen' + *upacāra* 'offering') a set of sixteen offerings for the deity

shraddha/*śraddhā:* faith, respect

Shrauta Sutra/*Śrautasūtra:* books dealing with Vedic religious matters

shravana/*śravana:* listening, hearing about the deity

shrivatsa/*śrīvatsa:* a curl of hair on Vishnu's chest

shruti/*śruti:* that which is 'heard'; the four Vedas

Shudra/*Śūdra:* the labor class; a person from this class

Shuka/*Śuka:* Vyasa's son

Shukra/*Śukra:* Venus and one of the planetary gods; the teacher of the demons

Shvetavaraha/*Śvetavārāha:* lit. the 'white boar's'; name of the current Kalpa or the present Brahmic day

Siddhi: success, realization; Ganesha's wife

Sita/*Sītā:* the heroine of the *Ramayana;* Rama's wife

Skanda: son of Shiva and Parvati, after whom the *Skanda Purana* is named
smarana/*smarana:* remembering, remembering the deity
Smriti/*Smrti:* that which is 'remembered'; the books or literature making up the Hindu code of conduct
snana/*snāna:* bath
Soma: the moon; the Moon god; a sacred drink of the Vedic times
srishti/*srsti:* creation, world, universe
Sudaman/*Sudāman:* a Brahmin classmate of Krishna; also *Sudāmā*
sukha: pleasure, happiness
Sumitra/*Sumitrā:* mother of Lakshmana and Shatrughna (in the *Ramayana)*
Sumukha: the 'beautiful-faced'; Ganesha's epithet
Surya/*Sūrya:* the Sun; the Sun god
Suta/*Sūta:* a narrator, storyteller, a sage
sutra/*sūtra:* string, thread, formula, aphorism
svaha/*svāhā:* a mystical word used for an oblation, as in the 'homa' ceremony
svastika: an auspicious symbol; also 'swastika'; a symbol for Ganesha
svastivachana/*svastivācana:* auspicious recitation
Svayambhuva/*Svāyambhuva:* lit. 'son of the self- born'; the first Manu

tamas: a *guna* or quality of the lowest (third) degree
tambula/*tāmbūla:* betel leaf
Tamradhvaja/*Tāmradhvaja:* son of Moradhvaja
tandava/*tāndava:* the cosmic dance of Shiva
Tantra: a non-Vedic tradition of mystic practices
Tapati/*Tapatī:* a daughter of the Sun god
Tarkshya/*Tārksya:* a deity; an epithet of Garuda, the eagle who is the vehicle for Vishnu
tilaka: a sacred mark made on the forehead with a powder or paste; also *tilak*
tithi: day of a lunar month
Treta Yuga: see yuga
Tripurari/*Tripurāri:* lit. the 'triple city's enemy' (*tri* 'three' + *pura* 'city' + *ari* 'enemy'); Shiva's epithet
Tungadhvaja/*Tungadhvaja:* a king

Ulkamukha/*Ulkāmukha:* a king

Uma/*Umā:* the Mother Goddess; Shiva's spouse, Durga
upachara/*upacāra:* service, treat, treatment, offering, means
Upanishad/*Upaniṣad:* the philosophical books attached to the Vedas
Upapurana/*Upapurāna:* any minor Purana
upavasa/*upavāsa:* fasting done for any purpose, especially for a worship
upavita/*upavīta:* sacred thread
upaya/*upāya:* solution, means

Vaikhanasa/*Vaikhānasa:* a Vaishnava tradition, its books
Vaikuntha/*Vaikuntha:* Vishnu's abode
Vaishnava/*Vaiṣṇava:* belonging to Vishnu; a Vaishnavite or devotee of
    Vishnu
Vaishya/*Vaiśya:* the business class; a person from this class
Vaivasvata: belonging to Vivasvat
Vallabha: a saint and philosopher of bhakti and non-dualism
Valmiki/*Vālmīki:* the original author of the *Ramayana*
Vamana/*Vāmana:* dwarf; the Dwarf incarnation of Vishnu
vanaprastha/*vānaprastha:* the third of the four stages of life; the retired life
vandana: bowing, praying to the deity
Varaha/*Varāha:* boar; the Boar incarnation of Vishnu
varna/*varna:* variation, distinction, sign, class, color
Varuna/*Varuna:* a Vedic god, a world guardian
Vasordhara/*Vasordhārā:* lit. 'stream of riches'; a small worship as part of
    a longer worship
Vastoshpati/*Vāstospati:* house lord, god of housing
vastra: cloth, clothes
Vasu: riches; also the gods known as the 'eight Vasus' associated with
    Indra and Vishnu
Vasudeva/*Vāsudeva:* lit. Vasudeva's son, Krishna, whose father's name is
    Vasudeva
Vasuki/*Vāsuki:* a divine serpent
vatsalya/*vātsalya:* parental affection, devotion with an affectionate attitude
Vayu/*Vāyu:* the 'wind' god
Veda: knowledge; the four books with the earliest Aryan literature in
    archaic Sanskrit or Vedic
Vedanga/*Vedāṅga:* a group of ancient Sanskrit books divided in six
    categories

Vedanta/*Vedānta:* the Upanishadic philosophy of non-dualism; lit. *Veda* 'knowledge' + *anta* 'end'

Vighnanasha/*Vighnanāśa:* the 'obstacle destroyer'; Ganesha's epithet

Vigraha: body of a deity in the form of an image

Vikata/*Vikata:* the 'tough' one; Ganesha's epithet

vina/*vīnā:* a musical string instrument

Vinayaka/*Vināyaka:* the 'distinguished leader'; Ganesha's epithet

visarjana: farewell to a deity

Vishnu/*Visnu:* Pervader; God, the Active

vishva/*viśva:* all, world, universe, cosmos

Vivasvat: vivifier, radiator; the Sun god

Vraja: the place where Krishna spent his early life; also *Braja (Braj, Brij* in Hindi)

vrata: vow, worship, commitment

Vyakarana/*Vyākarana:* grammar

Vyasa/*Vyāsa:* arranger, a sage believed to be the author of the *Mahabharata,* Puranas, etc.

yajamana/*yajamāna:* lit. 'one who does *yajña';* a worshipper

yajna/*yajña:* ceremony, sacrifice, Vedic ritual

Yajur Veda/*Yajurveda:* A Vedic book

Yama: the god of death

Yami/*Yamī:* a daughter of the Sun god and Yama's sister; the river Yamuna

Yamuna/*Yamunā:* a river

yantra: a geometrical design as mandala, machine, instrument

Yashoda/*Yaśoda:* foster mother of Krishna

Yudhishthira/*Yudhisthira:* the oldest brother among the Pandavas (in the *Mahabharata)*

yuga: a time unit, 'age' in cosmic time; the four yugas, namely *Satya, Tretā, Dvāpara,* and *Kali*

Bibliography

BABB, LAWRENCE A.
1975   *The Divine Hierarchy: Popular Hinduism in Central India.*
                New York: Columbia University Press.

BANERJEE, J. N.
1974   *The Development of Hindu Iconography.*   New Delhi:
                Munshiram Manoharlal.

BASHAM, A. L.
1959   *The Wonder That Was India.*   New York: Grove Press.

BHAKTIVEDANTA, SWAMI PRABHUPADA
1972-1980   *Śrīmad Bhāgavatam* (with translation of the *Bhagavata
                Purana*).   Cantos 1-10, 30 vols.   New York and Los
                Angeles: The Bhaktivedanta Book Trust.

BHARADWAJ, S.M.
1973   *Hindu Pilgrimage in India.*   Berkeley: University of
                California Press.

BHARATI, AGEHANANDA
1965   *The Tantric Tradition.* London: Rider and Company.

BHATTACHARJI, SUKUMARI
1970   *The Indian Theogony: A Comparative Study of Indian
                Mythology from the Vedas to the Puranas.*   Cambridge:
                Cambridge University Press.

BUHLER, GEORGE, trans.
1989   *The Laws of Manu.*   Sacred Books of the East, Vol. 25.
                London: Oxford University Press.

CHANDOLA, ANOOP
1982   *Mystic and Love Poetry of Medieval Hindi.*   New Delhi:
                Today and Tomorrow's Publishers.

DASGUPTA, SURENDRANATH
    1922-57   *A History of Indian Philosophy*, 5 vols.   Cambridge: Cambridge University Press.

DE, S. K.
    1963   *Sanskrit Poetics as a Study of Aesthetic.*   Berkeley: University of California Press.

DE BARRY, WILLIAM THEODORE, ed.
    1958   *Sources of Indian Tradition.*   New York: Columbia University Press.

DIMMITT, CORNELIA, and J. A. B. VAN BUITENEN, eds. and trans.
    1978   *Classical Hindu Mythology: A Reader in Sanskrit Puranas.* Philadelphia: Temple University Press.

DUMONT, LOUIS
    1970   *Homo Hierarchicus: The Caste System and Its Implications.* Chicago: University of Chicago Press.

ECK, DIANA L.
    1981   *Darśan: Seeing the Divine Image in India.* Chambersburg, Pennsylvania: Anima Publications.

EDGERTON, FRANKLIN, trans.
    1965   *The Bhagavad Gita.* New York: Harper and Row.

GRIFFITH, RALPH T. H., trans.
    1963   *Hymns of the Rig Veda*, 2 vols. Varanasi, India: The Chowkhamba Sanskrit Series.

HIRIYANNA, MYSORE
    1949   *The Essentials of Indian Philosophy.* London: Allen and Unwin.

HOPKINS, THOMAS J.
    1971   *The Hindu Religious Tradition.* Encino, California: Dickenson Publishing Company.

KANE, P. V.
    1930-1962   *History of Dharmaśāstra*, 5 vols. Pune, India: Bhandarkar
                     Oriental Research Institute.

KHANNA, MADHU
    1979   *Yantra: The Tantric Symbol of Cosmic Unity*. London:
                     Thames and Hudson.

KINSLEY, DAVID R.
    1982   *Hinduism: A Cultural Perspective*. Englewood Cliffs, New
                     Jersey: Prentice-Hall.

KRAMRISCH, STELLA
    1976   *The Hindu Temple*, 2 vols. Delhi: Motilal Banarasidass.

LINGAT, ROBERT
    1973   *The Classical Law of India*. Berkeley: University of
                     California Press.

MICHELL, GEORGE
    1977   *The Hindu Temple: An Introduction to Its Meaning and
                     Forms*. New York: Harper and Row.

MILLER, BARBARA STOLER, trans.
    1988   *The Bhagavad-Gita: Krishna's Counsel in Time of War*.
                     New York: Bantam Books.

MORGAN, KENNETH W., ed.
    1963   *The Religion of the Hindus*. New York: The Ronald Press.

O'FLAHERTY, WENDY DONIGER, trans.
    1981   *The Rig Veda: An Anthology*. Harmondsworth, Middlesex,
                     England: Penguin Books.

    1984   *Hindu Myths*. Harmondsworth, Middlesex, England:
                     Penguin Books.

PARRINDER, GEOFFREY
    1982   *Avatar and Incarnation: A Comparison of Indian and
                     Christian Beliefs*. New York: Oxford University Press.

RADHAKRISHNAN, S.
    1940   *Indian Philosophy*. London: Allen and Unwin.

    1953   *The Principle Upanisads*. London: Allen and Unwin.

ROY, PRATAP CHANDRA, trans.
    1927-1932   *The Mahabharata*, 11 vols. Calcutta: Oriental Publishing
                    Company.

SHASTRI, HARI PRASAD, trans.
    1952-1959   *The Ramayana of Valmiki*, 3 vols. London: Shantisadan.

SINHA, NANDLAL, trans.
    1974   *The Bhakti Sutras of Narada*. The sacred Books of the
                    Hindus Series, Vol. 7, Pt. 1. New York: AMS Press.

SINGER, MILTON
    1969   *Krishna: Myths, Rites and Attitudes*. Chicago: University
                    of Chicago Press.

SKANDA-PURANA (Sanskrit Text, 7 vols.)
    n.d.   Calcutta: Vangavasi Press.

VAN BUITENEN, J. A. B., trans.
    1973-(incomplete) *The Mahabharata*. Chicago: University of Chicago Press.

WAGHORNE, JOANNE PUNZO and NORMAN CUTLER
    1984   *Gods of Flesh/Gods of Stone*. Chambersburg, Pennsylvania:
                    Anima Publications.

WINTERNITZ, MORIZ
    1963   *A History of Indian Literature*. New York: Harper and
                    Row.

ZIMMER, HEINRICH
    1962   *Myths and Symbols in Indian Art and Civilization*. New
                    York: Harper and Row.

Index

Adityas, 26, 84
Aesthetic experience, 46
Altruism, 3, 104
Alvars, 49
ananda, 46, 47
Anushtubh (meter), 13
Aryans, 2, 7
Artistic expression, 47
Ashramas, 11
Ashtadhyai, 9
Atman, 43, 44
Austrics, 8, 49
Austro-asiatics, 8
Ayodhya, 32

Badrinath, 31, 35
Being, 1
bhakti rasa, 46, 47
Big Egg (*Virāj*), 88
Bhilla Guharaja, *See* Guha
Brahman, 37, 43, 44, 77, 93
Brahmanda, 39
Brahma-nirvana, 44
Breath regulatory exercise, 74
Buddha, 10, 11, 32, 78

Chemical changes, 47
Christ, 32
Civil disobedience, 1
Collectivism, 3
Cosmic ocean (sea), 2, 28, 83
Cosmogonic hymn, 87
Culture hero, 9, 10

Dasharatha, 48, 50, 68
Devotion emotion. *See bhakti rasa*
dhoti, 75
Dipavali, 21

Dualism, 37
dukha, 43, 46
Durga Puja, 24
Dramatic science, 46
Dravidians, 8, 49
dvaita, 37
Dwaraka (Dvaraka), 31

Earth, 75, 78
Emotions, 46
Emotional approach, 47
Enlightened self-interest, 3
Ethical socialism, 3

Fast (*upavasa*), 75
Fecundity, 81
Fertility, 81
Fertilization, 2, 102
Festival of Lights. *See Dipavali*
Fluid secretion, 46
Forefathers, 84
Fructification, 2, 81, 102

Gandhi, Mahatma, 1, 2, 32
Ganesha Chaturthi, 23
Ganges, 24
Garuda, 30, 77
gayatri, 26, 84
Germination, 81
Goals of life, 11, 42
gotra, 78
Grahas, 28, 29
Guha, 48, 49, 50, 104
guru puja, 35

Harmonious balance, 3
Hatha Yoga, 74
Healing fluids, 47

137

About the Author

ANOOP CHANDOLA was born in the Himalayas to a Hindu priestly family. He holds degrees from the universities of Allahabad, Lucknow, California (Berkeley), and Chicago. His doctorate from the University of Chicago is in linguistics. He has taught at the universities of California, Washington, Texas, and Wisconsin, and in India at Sardar Vallabhbhai Patel University and the M.S. University at Baroda. Currently he is a professor in the East Asian Studies Department at the University of Arizona. With both priestly and scholarly knowledge of Sanskrit, Professor Chandola has pursued teaching and research in Hindu religion, philosophy, culture and literature. Several of his books and articles are related to Hinduism, including *Mystic and Love Poetry of Medieval Hindi* (1982) and an article, "On Practical Hinduism: The Puja as Human Contact" in *The Mankind Quarterly*, Summer, 1989.